AF399998

Tales of Melodies

Maher Asaad Baker

Fuad Al-Qrize

CONTENTS

INTRODUCTION

Latvia's small Baltic space with its culturally vibrant atmosphere leads people to marvel at its complex musical heritage that casts magic on audiences throughout the world. The Latvian musical domain creates an elegant artistic ensemble because multiple artistic elements work harmoniously throughout this symphonic national journey.

Ancient musical spells occupying Latvian green fields and ancient oak forests since antiquity form the fundamental origins of all Latvian musical creativity. Traditional pastoral elements emanating from natural energies within eternal human experience cycles create musical elegance which remains pure through unmodified traditional melody sounds. Powdered notes escaping from rural home chimneys let listeners experience a wholesome lyricism even though these innocent melodies express deep emotional power for the heart.

Latvian musicians in the modern era show absolute alignment to modernist radical principles by displaying avant-garde revolutionary elements in their work. Adventurous musicians develop unconventional approach to music through fresh musical signatures to break natural audibility conventions and traditional harmonic structures. The experimental research into electronic sounds, microtones and chance procedures has led these composers to generate paranormal audio effects which transcend standard communication methods in music.

This perfect fusion of traditional elements with experimental artistic techniques reveals the core definition of Latvian musical Gesamtkunstwerk which celebrates ancient traditions in its symphonic high point during an advancing era of creative exploration. As a lasting and constant development this chromatic composition represents an eternal tribute to human endurance that keeps Latvia strong through its historical hardships toward the pursuit of ultimate aesthetic beauty.

Latvia reveals its sacred traditional heritage through musical sanctuaries that have survived all centuries since the beginning of time. The melodic voice of the kokle creates mournful sounds like a zither through its chordophone body as it joins Latvian chanting traditions guided by eerie polyphonic harmonies that are descended from Finno-Ugric and Baltic heritage sounds. Throughout history these interminable musical intervals have served as life-force for both musicians and tonalists in

Latvia. The natural universe and terran sustenance provided a fertile environment for these musical forms which originated from its abundant space.

Latvia's foremost ethnomusicologists devote their entire life to sacramentally develop the detailed documentation of Latvian traditional music since they honor its ancient musical heritage above all else through their precise scientific method. Through their tireless efforts they defended promissory cultural heritage as well as serving as an eternal muse for contemporary artists to explore traditional sources for original artwork.

The successful artistic path of this distinct nation shows respect for former mystical traditions and seeks to advance artistic boundaries. As a traditional artistic trend it remains eternal yet it continually undergoes modifications to become this force of human survival which uplifts relentless human determination to succeed artistically no matter what the conditions are.

The binding element of Latvian folk music embodies the country's choral tradition since this practice has developed into the cornerstone of the national musical legacy. Letting the human voice and collective power guide them the Latvian choral movement has

---

produced successful choirs together with skilled conductors who now perform both nationally and internationally.

The Latvian Radio Choir holds worldwide recognition through its presentation of traditional and modern choral music that displays Latvian vocalists' high level of skill. Through its precise control of cappella singing and partnerships with famous composers the choir has become Latvia's cultural representative in musical expressions.

Latvian instrumental music together with choral tradition continues to develop its own distinct

---

identity through the exceptional talents of both composers and instrumental performers. For more than a century the Latvian National Symphony Orchestra has established itself as a cultural institution through its constant delivery of breathtaking musical performances which demonstrate Latvia's cultural talent in music.

The orchestra plays Latvian composers' masterpieces under distinguished conductors who perform both romantic works by Jānis Ivanovs and avant-garde pieces by Pēteris Vasks. The cultural masterpiece collection of Latvia continues to gain international recognition which establishes Latvia as a vital force in worldwide classical music development.

Pianists from Latvia form an exemplary heritage which maintains strong influence over musicians worldwide. Latvian pianists through performers such as Vestards Šimkus and Georgs Pelēcis prove their mastery of using the piano to express authentic Latvian artistic essence through their technical abilities and emotional depth.

Through their musical performances these pianists continue to promote Latvian composers worldwide by actively advocating for their musical works. The Riga Piano

Competitions together with other prestigious piano competitions serve as platforms to develop future Latvian master pianists which strengthens the country's position as a global center of musical talent excellence.

Latvia has maintained its classic musical tradition while simultaneously developing new contemporary music styles which express its changing cultural heritage. The return of Latvian folk music during recent decades under the leadership of Ieva Akuratere and Laima Jansone added contemporary elements to traditional musical structures so both Latvian and international audiences could appreciate it.

Today's folk musicians bring traditional instrument sounds of the kokle and others into new popularity by uniting them with modern production techniques and maverick musical structures. Modern musicians make a magical blend of ancient Latvian music heritage which remains vital because of their innovative work.

Latvian music has experienced two concurrent advancements: Folksinger achievements and the emergence of young composers who expand classical composition possibilities. International acclaim has welcomed composers Santa Ratniece and Andris Dzenītis who produce innovative site-based works derived from Latvian natural and cultural elements.

The ethereal character with meditative elements and strong geographical integration in compositions by these Latvian composers has gained nationwide acclaim marking Latvia as a center of avant-garde classical music.

The contemporary music scene in Latvia shows remarkable strength because popular music has regained its popularity in the last few years. The nation's musical prodigies have succeeded worldwide in both Latvian pop rock and electronic music space.

International audiences now recognize the

artists Brainstorm along with the moving pop ballads of Kristīne Prauliņa as representatives of distinctive Latvian popular music.

The growth of music festivals and events which include Positivus Festival and the Saulkrasti Jazz Festival gives Latvian artists established and upcoming musicians opportunities to present their music to diverse audiences. These cultural spots create both an active domestic music establishment and intercultural links that connect Latvian performers directly with artists from across the globe resulting in enriched musical compositions in the country.

The Latvian musical tradition continues to thrive through the establishment of renowned musical learning institutions especially the Jāzeps Vītols Latvian Academy of Music that breeds talented musicians and composers across many generations.

Educational institutions succeed in developing technical excellence while developing students' understanding of the culturally distinct musical messages in Latvian works. Students who graduate from these prestigious music schools continue making major musical impacts worldwide thus establishing Latvia as a country with highly accomplished musicians.

Latvia's musical voice functions as an enduring testimony to artistic transformation through art as the world faces perpetual shifts of information and musical evolution. The music created by this tiny country has established a long-lasting heritage that presently holds audiences worldwide spellbound showing human beings can continuously express their creativity while creating meaningful cultural impacts.

Latvian ethnomusicologists lead their professional lives dedicated to thorough musical heritage documentation and academic research of traditional Latvian songs. Latvian folk music survives because intangible cultural

---

wealth protection efforts of tireless researchers ensures both its musical value remains clear and its influence continues to motivate creative musicians today.

Latvian artists within this established home have created a new scene where they merge folk music with modern ideas. Their strong identity with their culture and a desire to be creative discourages them from following common music genres.

People worldwide honor Ieva Akuratere for her outstanding renditions of Latvian folk music that have become widely recognized. Akuratere fuses the kokle's oldest traditions with modern methods and unique ideas to connect with both people who appreciate old and those who enjoy innovative music.

Laima Jansone combines ancient Latvian musical ideas with modern art skills in her original compositions. With her unique approach, Jansone has returned traditional Latvian dainas to the spotlight for today's listeners to appreciate their beauty in new arrangements.

Their influence is not limited to folk music, as they have contributed much to the way music is created in Latvia now. The influence of folk singers has encouraged others to try different blends of tradition and creativity, creating a vibrant environment for all forms of art.

These different groups of musicians have started creating music that mixes Latvian folk melodies with the latest ideas from modern composers, such as Smāra has done. Ultimately, the album creates an enchanting mix of sounds that makes it hard to classify and encourages listeners to engage in a unique experience that exists outside these boundaries.

Besides folk-style experiments, the Latvian musical world is home to a flourishing of contemporary classical music that reflects the nation's rich heritage. Santa Ratniece and Andris Dzenītis, both highly regarded Latvian composers, have attracted people from all over the world with their site-connected compositions that represent Latvia's beautiful nature and age-old traditions.

You can hear the ethereal sound and meditative qualities in Ratniece's compositions, which encourage listeners to travel toward a state where body and soul are unified. However, Dzenītis has been commended for mixing traditional Latvian instruments with contemporary compositional methods to build music that reflects Latvia's culture and the changes happening in today's world.

Because of these collaborative music ventures, Latvia has become recognized worldwide as a leader in artistic development. Success internationally enjoyed by Latvian musicians and composers is evidence that a blend of culture and modern days can bring about meaningful changes.

The balance between the past and the future is seen in the lively popular music scene now present in Latvia. People like Kristīne Prauliņa, whose refined and reflective pop ballads have taken over the world, and Brainstorm, the group consisting of two musicians, who first used Latvian-based sounds in electronic music, have blended modern art with Latvian traditions.

Because of the success of Latvian artists, more music festivals and concerts have sprung up around the country, giving a chance for everyone from leading stars to rising musicians to share their talents with people from different backgrounds. Because of festivals like Positivus and the Saulkrasti Jazz Festival, Latvian musicians now have the chance to play with foreign musicians and add new influences to their musical scene.

Because of the significant input by their graduates to the world of music, Latvia is now widely regarded as a place with plenty of bright musical talent. Leading Latvian pianists on the concert platforms and gifted classical composers from Latvia have helped keep the nation's music vibrant and inspire people across the globe.

Amid today's changing world, combining Latvian folk music with new sounds demonstrates the positive impact of sharing cultures and how creativity remains in people. Thanks to the balance of rooted tradition and artistic inspiration, music in the country inspires us by highlighting how music joins people, promotes awareness, and shows the beauty in shared human life.

Folk music from Latvia, famous for its touching notes and lively rhythms, has played a key role in developing the nation's unique culture. After being a key part of everyday life in rural communities, these old styles of music have now come to define Latvian heritage and show the strong and flexible souls of the Latvian people.

As Latvian artists have become successful, more music festivals and concerts have appeared around the country, giving both well-known and unknown musicians an opportunity to perform for people from various communities. Thanks to such festivals as Positivus and the Saulkrasti Jazz Festival, Latvian musicians get to work with artists from all over the globe, making Latvian music richer.

Latvia is now known for having a lot of talented musicians thanks to the many contributions by its graduates. World-renowned performers and composers from Latvia have worked hard to keep the country's music alive and exciting for people across the globe.

Merging Latvian folk songs with modern sounds shows that sharing similarities between cultures encourages creativity. The mixture of cultural heritage and new creativity allows music in the nation to inspire us by underlining how music knits people together, informs us, and exhibits the beauty found in sharing life.

Thanks to its moving melodies and lively rhythms, Latvian folk music has influenced the country's special character in significant ways. Being a staple in rural areas, these styles of traditional music are now recognized as an imperative part of Latvian identity and highlight how strong and pliable those in Latvia can be.

Because Latvian artists have become successful, there are now more music festivals and concerts in the country, allowing both well-known and new musicians to share their talents with different communities. As a result of Positivus and the Saulkrasti Jazz Festival, Latvian musicians collaborate with artists from many different places, enriching Latvian music.

The many talented musicians in Latvia can be attributed to its graduates and what they have done. Accepted internationally, Latvian performers and composers are dedicated to keeping their country's music interesting for listeners worldwide.

Bringing Latvian folk music together with modern tunes demonstrates that cultures can work together to generate new artistic ideas. The combination of old traditions and new ways of creating music in the nation encourages us by highlighting how it connects people, informs them, and displays the joy that comes from living together.

The special character of Latvia is shaped in part by the evocative melodies and lively rhythms found in Latvian folk music. Because these musical styles started in rural areas, they are now seen as vital to Latvian heritage and reflect the strength and flexibility of Latvians.

As a result, Latvian people are encouraged to shape their shared values and traditions through choral singing, a practice handed down by previous generations. Many choral competitions and festivals around the country, like the Latvian National Song and Dance Festival, allow this respected tradition to thrive and keep moving forward.

Even though folk and choral music have the most influence, music is important in Latvia for several other reasons as well. Recently, the popularity of various music styles in the country has helped it become known internationally and become an important part of its cultural story.

Singer Kristīne Prauliņa, whose moving pop songs have won her popularity everywhere, and electronic duo Brainstorm, who mix Latvian heritage into their unique and adventurous music, have managed to combine elements of their culture with modern creativity. These artists have pleased people with their performances and represented Latvia in many parts of the world.

Music festivals and events in Latvia, such as the Positivus Festival and the Saulkrasti Jazz Festival, have played a big part in keeping music as a strong symbol of the nation's culture. They have not only allowed local musicians to flourish but also given Latvian artists the chance to interact with various audiences, both from within the country and abroad, building stronger connections for Latvia and displaying its own cultural style.

This active and ever-changing musical scene is possible in part because important institutions such as the Jāzeps Vītols Latvian Academy of Music are committed to training new musicians and keeping the nation's traditions alive. Such schools have helped their students gain expertise and also made sure they value the stories in Latvian music, ensuring the country's musical character keeps being felt and developed over time.

Latvian music art shows not only who Latvians are but is also central to what defines them. Over the years, music has helped unite the people, allowed them to challenge injustice, and promoted Latvian values and aspirations, strengthening the nation's history and image worldwide.

Latvian music proves that great art can transform and link people, moving past obstacles to increase our understanding of humanity.

While we face the constant changes of the 21st century, the lasting impact of music on Latvian culture makes it clear that creative expression benefits the nation and brings people together. In this deep and inspiring music from Latvia, we see both a love for the country's history and a sign of what can happen when we use our traditions to inspire great progress in the future.

THE ROOTS

Folk music in Latvia began to develop as early as the Neolithic era, when the first farmers started to live in permanent settlements. Our ancient ancestors started forming a stronger bond with the environment at this important period, which later appeared in their music as a basic and powerful quality.

Early people in Latvia, as revealed by

archaeology, began with simple percussive tools, for example, drums and rattles, that were all made from natural materials like wood, bone, and animal hides. The music from these early instruments built the first steps needed for creating more elaborate tunes. The drums and musical instruments they used would have reverberated through the ancient forests and fields, uniting these first settlers.

In the Bronze Age, Latvian music started to become more refined than it was during the Stone Age. Metalworking and dividing society into different classes introduced a new age of cultural life, where older myths and legends were mixed into new musical styles.

Many tales of the early era were passed verbally, describing the achievements of great heroes, the awards of gods, and the marvels seen in the natural world. The epic stories, full of symbolism and metaphor, were expressed through the music and harmonies found in Latvian minds. The melancholy sound and repetitive tuning of these old ballads highlight the strong link between the Latvian people and where they came from, as they dealt with hardship and joys over the centuries.

With the Iron Age beginning, the Latvians went through many changes, and their music became quite different. The appearance of new ways to organize society, the growth of trade, and the arrival of various cultural groups all led to the development of a more advanced language for music.

During this time, Latvian folk music started to use polyphonic structures, meaning that several different melodies were weaved together to create something rich and harmonious. The increased use of polyphony could have been caused by the musical practices of neighboring peoples, along with development in Latvian musical instruments.

Latvian music gained new variations in sound

and style because of the introduction of the kokle zither and the development of wooden trumpets called taure. The use of these instruments introduced new variations in harmonies and melodies, helping the early development of Latvian folk music's choral traditions.

The traditional beliefs of paganism strongly influenced the development of Latvian folk music. Like other Baltic and Finno-Ugric people, the Latvian people were directly connected to the natural world and the gods that were thought to control its balance.

Sacred and mystical elements gave the music from this period its special character, with chants, incantations, and ritual songs being essential in Latvian religious ceremonies. Traditions regarding the sun, moon, forests, and waters were expressed in the complex structure of tunes, beats, and words, resulting in a musical form that connected everyday life with the world above.

The use of the kantele in their music was typical, since it was thought to be capable of attracting the attention of the gods. The soft and somber sounds of the kantele were necessary in religious ceremonies, birth and death rites, and group gatherings, making the music more spiritual and sacred.

The further the Latvian people developed, their musical culture began to blend with the well-established poetry found in the region. Latvian folk music was largely built on the dainas, which are short verses telling the wisdom, beliefs, and personal stories of the Latvian people.

Because these poems were handed down through generations, first in speech and later in writing, they became the basis for musical compositions ranging from simple folk music to grand choral pieces. The way the Latvian language is spoken influenced the dainas to have consistent melodies and rhythms, making the music sound unified and natural.

As Christianity appeared in the area known as the Baltic region and reached the Latvians, the way they played music was greatly affected. While folk music was mainly influenced by pagan traditions for hundreds of years, Christian hymns and religious chants began having a strong effect on it.

Using Christian symbols and concepts in music helped the Latvian people gradually accept and adopt their new faith. Nonetheless, instead of merely choosing the songs and music used by Christians, the Latvian people incorporated these new pieces into their traditional folk music, merging their old culture with the effects of Christianity.

In Latvian folk music, the organ was used more often, and its impressive sounds blended with other common instruments to form a full, fascinating musical texture. Adding hymns and sacred chants to Latvian repertoires made it possible for sounds of worship from Christianity to mingle with those from the ancient pagan spiritual past.

With time, Latvian folk music has adjusted to different periods in history, but it has remained true to its original spirit. The Arabesque melodies of the Neolithic world, the complex songs of the Iron Age, and the rich prayers of every faith have built an impressive cultural thread that has stayed as strong as Latvia's very earth for centuries.

Today, people all over the world continue to appreciate the unique melodies and rhythms of Latvian folk music, which represents how human creativity and the strong spirit of Latvians last over time.

With their memorable pictures, imaginative metaphors, and themes, dainas have lasted in Latvian culture, underlining the value of using spoken and sung words. Bringing poetry and musical traditions together has formed a musical history for Latvia that is strongly connected with its roots and with the present day.

The distinctive 4/4 or 6/8 meter in dainas has created a variety of Latvian folk songs, from songs meant for dancing to those that express deep thoughts. Since the sound of dainas is modeled on Latvian speech patterns, they have become part of the nation's music, forming a tight bond between recitation and singing.

Dainas are significant for more than their rhythm, as they have inspired many melodies found in Latvian music. Dainas are full of images, literary metaphors, and age-old ideas that express the prevailing emotions and dreams of the Latvian people.

Dainas include songs of joy and appreciation, as well as those that reflect the sadness and problems of people. Thanks to their meaningful feelings and Latvian culture, dainas have become a reflection of the Latvian people rather than just poetry.

The legacy of dainas goes past solo or instrumental music, as they have also made a deep contribution to the development of Latvia's choral tradition. Polychronic dainas, featuring many melodies and harmonies, create a foundation for Latvia's most famous choral works.

For many years, composers have arranged dainas into beautiful choral works, so the individual poems merge into a chorus of sounds. It becomes an energetic and expressive portrait of Latvia, reflecting how the community and individual stories are closely linked.

The deep connection between Latvian choral music and dainas has made it a well-known aspect of the country's culture, as the voice is capable of expressing deep and meaningful ideas. Both the large, impressive daina performances on state stages and the small local choirs preserve the music and word craft of Latvian dainas.

Even though dainas started as personal poems, their lasting position in Latvian culture is truly significant. There was a long tradition in Latvia of teaching dainas to younger generations by speaking them, rooted in the Latvian culture.

For example, these short songs, which often rhyme and are delivered spontaneously or changed for the situation, at first were not part of music designed for presentations. However, they mainly saved and handed down the Latvian people's culture, ideas, and life stories to future generations.

The dainas started to be documented and organized only in the 19th century, due to the influence of the Latvian national awakening and the involvement of scholars and folklorists. As a result of their efforts, Kvīps and Rancāns compiled the acclaimed "Latvian Folksongs," which held onto Latvian dainas, ultimately making their way into developing Latvian musical styles.

As the Latvian nation faced the challenges of recent history, the importance of dainas has grown. Now, these folk songs are played and prized by many Latvian composers, musicians, and performers, who want to guarantee that this valued tradition does not fade.

In classical music, dainas have acted as inspiration for many works, from large, joyful orchestral pieces to quiet, intimate choral writings. Emīls Dārziņš and Jānis Mediņš have musically incorporated the structures of Latvian folk songs, so their music reaches a blend of tradition and pioneering ideas.

As well, the dainas have become part of Latvia's lively modern music community, with artists from many genres trying to rework and enliven these ancient songs. Both singer-songwriters and experimental composers still use dainas as a source of inspiration for their music.

Because Latvian music has spread to many places globally, the dainas have become important in introducing Latvian poetry and music to international audiences. Many international choirs, orchestras, and ensembles have local musicians sing dainas in concert halls and at festivals, attracting listeners with the emotional power and age-old beauty that are in these verses.

Due to how every piece of this tradition can be understood across languages and cultures, remarkable collaborative works have been created to give dainas a bigger audience. Artists in Latvia have teamed up with those from other countries, blending their traditional songs with music from other places, resulting in a unique mix of cultural art and sounds.

It is impossible to understate how important the dainas are in shaping Latvian music. Because of the unique language and rhythm of their poems, Latvians have been able to save their traditions, knowledge, and beliefs and also give rise to a varied musical heritage.

No matter if the dainas are lively folk music or elegant, choral music, they continue to flow throughout Latvian songs, showing how important words are in music. As Latvia has experienced tough periods in its history, the dainas have continued to hold the people together, guide them towards their roots, and help them express their rich and emotional poetry.

At the start, Latvian folk music was based on instruments such as wooden, bone, and animal hide drums and rattles, forming its beginning. The early instruments, created by the earth's beating, blended with the yearly cycles of nature and helped people meet the powerful forces all around them.

As time passed, Latvian music started to reflect nature more and more. With the introduction of the kantele and the taure, both new types of instruments, Finnish music started to use more complex melodic and harmonic patterns. Despite the broadening scope of music in Latvia, the link to the rhythms found in nature remained constant.

You can see how important nature is to Latvians by how their music is influenced by every season. For many years, Latvian musicians have drawn ideas and inspiration from the yearly cycle of spring, summer, autumn, and winter.

Springtime melodies in Latvia are cheerful and heartfelt, reflecting how the people appreciate the renewal that spring brings with its coming. The lively songs, played while stomping your feet and clapping your hands, stand for the Latvian people's respect for nature and its ability to awaken after winter.

As summer comes, Latvian music grows gentle and lyrical, playing songs with melodies and harmonies reminiscent of scorching days in the countryside and after-harvest times. During summer, Latvians often add musical instruments like the kokle and taure, whose thoughtful tones mirrors the quiet beauty of the ripened season.

The onset of autumn and the slow end of farming are observed in the gentler, elegiac music of Latvia. The use of minor keys and cold harmonies during the winter is a touching pointer to the fact that everything in life and nature moves in cycles.

When winters come, the music reflects on spiritual subjects and ritual songs become very important for Latvians in protecting their traditions and honoring nature's hidden forces.

Besides the strong effects of seasons on Latvian music, the regular cycles of farm life have strongly influenced the musical culture. Because of how much the Latvian people love their homeland, their music is filled with great respect for nature and the routines used in farming.

Throughout the agricultural year, from preparing the land in spring to the autumn harvest, various Latvian songs express the people's joy and experiences. The sound of growing seasons is noticed in folk and choral songs, which use a strong rhythm to show the effort people put into farming.

In the end, moods in Latvian music grow more cheerful, with tunes that showcase the land's wealth and prosperity. Dainas, little verses that rhyme in Latvian music, commonly use strong images and metaphors to sing about the riches of the earth and their connection with nature.

There is a noticeable influence of tasks like raising animals or making goods from natural materials in Latvian music. These daily activity rhythms and sounds have been used in many folk songs and choral works, making the music as diverse and interesting as the farming rhythms that have supported the Latvian community for so long.

In Latvian music, a great respect for the natural world and the unknowns that control its rhythms can always be found. Latvians have always tried to interact with god through music, starting with their old pagan beliefs and continuing with newer expressions that include spiritual

Christianity.

Taking up a large part in traditional ceremonies, the kantele was regarded by the Latvians as a special instrument that could invite the gods to listen. Thanks to its unique sound, this instrument has helped make several types of musical works, from ancient pagan chants to religious hymns, appear sacred and meaningful for many.

In Latvian folk music, spiritual meaning is common, especially in the dainas that often use imagery and metaphors to venerate nature and the divinities who, it was believed, controlled natural processes.

Many Latvian songs praise the sun, the moon, the forests, and the waters, trying to capture the unusual forces that influence our lives. Because Latvians value and respect nature so much, their music often reflects a feeling of honor and wonder, and these beliefs have helped preserve their cultural and religious identity.

Over centuries, the development of Latvian music has kept its strong bond with nature, which attracts listeners from all over the world. Because of the strong influence of agriculture, the rhythms, tunes, and chords crafted on themes of the seasons continue to speak to listeners everywhere about the lasting power of the human spirit.

Latvian choirs have become known worldwide for their lush harmonies and moving versions of the dainas, leading to the country's music being regarded with admiration and fostering connections with musicians from many cultures. When choral pieces, rich with the sound of a kantele, are performed, audiences can be carried away and feel connected with others who share a similar experience, no matter where they come from.

Likewise, there has been a surge of contemporary Latvian musicians, who are working to renew the country's musical heritage by mixing traditional folk songs with modern music styles. You can enjoy the music's unique perspective, sparking an international audience's interest in nature and the universe, through these captivating, different type of works.

THE SOUL

From sad songs on missing love to upbeat songs about falling in love, folk music can portray the complete range of human feelings. The short, rhyming dainas form the basis of Latvian music and abound with powerful imagery and metaphors about traditional themes of love and desire. All the sorrow of wanting a loved one back, the distress of not being close, and the pleasing pain of envy are expressed with meaning and emotion in these poems, so they resonate with anyone.

The feelings of love in Latvian folk songs are not limited to romantic feelings. They also focus on the strong and meaningful family ties that have long played a key role in Latvian culture, using songs of comfort to mothers and fathers, brothers and sisters, and children, to shape a musical picture of love and family.

Throughout Latvian folk music, there is a strong respect for nature and the regular patterns in its changes. The tradition of Latvian music, from early drums to choral music of today, always included deep respect and admiration for the land, the seas, and the stars that have influenced the Latvian people.

Since Latvian folk music is inspired by the seasons, farming, and the impermanent changes in nature, its tunes and melodies capture the changes happening in the world around us. All these compositions show how much the Latvian people respect and appreciate nature.

In Latvian folk music, nature is honored in a way that moves past simply illustrating its patterns and movements. Because these pieces reflect real faith in the forces that influence our lives, they use images and symbols to honor the gods and spirits believed to control nature.

Throughout Latvian folk music, the idea of supernatural tales is woven in, taking inspiration from the country's rich myths and stories. From the eerie, lyrical notes of the folk instrument kantele, which might capture the gods' attention, to the deep chants and magical incantations, Latvian music has always had a spiritual feel to it.

Lyrical dainas mention depictions of gods and

supernatural beings very often because they were important to early Latvian traditions. In these verses, the sun, moon, forests, and water are held in deep respect, and their influence can clearly be seen.

Mythology's influence and mystery go further than the inclusion of fantastic characters. We often notice in Latvian folk songs a reflection on the relationship between humans and gods, accompanied by music that tries to unite these two worlds. In particular, the soft, otherworldly sounds of the kantele were trusted to attract the gods and turn the scene into something reverent.

Regardless of its ups and downs, Latvian music was strongly influenced by the themes of myth and the mysteries of life. Even when Christianity spread, ancient pagan traditions continued to be part of Latvian folk culture, making their way into stories and celebrations to highlight the lasting effect of the supernatural on ordinary people.

Examining the rich traditions of Latvian folk music shows that the themes and motifs found in these songs are linked together and cannot exist separately. All these different aspects of emotions and ideas about goddesses and church are held together, which explains the depth of the Latvian human experience.

Some love songs make use of images and ideas from nature, illustrating how our emotions and the cycles in nature are closely linked. In a similar way, there is usually an element of mystery in Latvian folk music, as it reflected the Latvian people's respect for the deities and spirits believed to control everything in the universe.

It shows the intricacy and depth of the Latvian folk music tradition, as well as the broad ideas it aims to share about people everywhere. Harmonies and melodies, paired with lyrics and imagery, reflect what we feel inside and show our relationship with nature and spirituality.

Exploring the past of Latvian folk music, we see over and over again that humans have used music and lyrics as a way to express themselves. No matter their origin, from the pounding beats of traditional drums to the rich choral music of recent times, these works praise the endurance and adaptability of Latvia's culture, attracting and exciting crowds worldwide.

The commonality found in Latvian folk music can be seen in different cultures and regions. The main ideas in these works – love, glory in nature, stories of mythology, and mystery – touch deep feelings universal among listeners.

The dainas, the heart of the Latvian musical tradition, are especially able to move people across cultures because of their colorful imagery and poetic language. The lyrics of the dainas, regardless of topic, often bring about a feeling of oneness that can be felt even today and in faraway countries.

It isn't only through song lyrics that Latvian folk music is universal; the same can be seen in its many compositions and musical structures. Because of their haunting, shimmering sound, and instrumental music, along with the choral polyphony, Finnish music can access the most basic human emotions and feelings.

Interest in preserving and promoting Latvian folk music is spearheaded by prominent folklorists whose wide-ranging researches have greatly helped how the world recognizes and cherishes this unique heritage.

One of the top contributors to Latvian Folklore is Krišjānis Barons, who is known as the "Father of Latvian Folklore" and spent his life collecting and organizing the popular Latvian folk songs that everyone knows and loves. In the late 1800s, the barons went across Latvia to obtain these poems or songs directly from the towns where they were sung or spoken.

The pinnacle of Barons' work was publishing the huge collection of "Latvian Folksongs," carefully gathering details on over 217,000 dainas. This one-of-a-kind work protected Latvian poetry and inspired countless songs that played a role in building the nation's music tradition.

But their lasting achievement was not limited only to the collection of these poems. Tallinn helped make the Latvian folk song tradition recognized as a main part of the national identity, which was significant for Latvia's national awakening.

Together with Krišjānis Barons, devoted folklorists and ethnomusicologists have done a lot to protect and research Latvian folk music. Thanks to people such as Anna Bētiņa and Emilis Melngailis, the Latvian musical tradition has survived and grown stronger through the generations.

Although the achievements of the Latvian folklorists have helped preserve the nation's musical traditions, it is the village singers who have truly kept the legacy alive.

For generations, these heroes have kept the

songs and chants of Latvian folk music intact by passing them on to their descendants, preserving the musical heritage of Latvia. Many times, village singers perform privately and have helped to maintain and grow the music and lyrics of Latvia.

These village singers are very important, since it is their constant commitment and detailed knowledge that have kept folk music alive during tough times in history. Even with great political and cultural turmoil, those dedicated to Latvian music have made sure that their nation's musical traditions continue to reach each generation.

One example of a village singer is Marija Reizniece, an important figure for Latvian folklore and music who has helped preserve the region's special music styles. Reizniece from the Latvian region of Vidzeme made it her life's mission to protect the traditional songs of her homeland by preserving them in written records and singing them for others to hear.

Thanks to Marija Reizniece and other talented individuals who worked so hard, the role of the village singer was preserved and grew to be very important in Latvia's cultural revival, inspiring more musicians in the process.

Besides the scholars of folk music and the local singers who have maintained the tradition, composers and conductors have helped Latvian music reach and excite audiences around the world.

Jānis Cimze has played an important role in developing Latvia's choral music traditions. As an important musician, Cimze used his skills to keep Latvian folk songs alive and to make their ancient harmony and richness stand out in new arrangements.

Under his leadership, Latvia's choral tradition flourished, and people both at home and

---

abroad were amazed by the strong and emotive ways the choirs sang the folk music of the country. Not only did Cimze preserve the musical culture of Latvia, but he helped bring it to many countries, sharing its distinctive music with the rest of the world.

Even so, Jānis Cimze's legacy is not limited to his skills as a conductor and arranger. Cimze used his teaching to help many generations of singers, encouraging them to respect and defend the traditions of Latvian folk music. Many of Cimze's trainees played leading roles in choral singing, each one keeping the spirit of the master alive and making sure Latvian music flourished over the years.

Next to Jānis Cimze, a group of prominent choral leaders have contributed greatly to Latvian music. The cultural legacy is growing stronger and more meaningful thanks to conductors such as Māris Sirmais, whose fusion of ancient folk melodies and current musical styles, and Sigvards Kļava, who has devotedly supported the Latvian choral tradition across the world.

With generations of changes in Latvian music, many talented composers and artists have appeared, working hard to refresh and update the nation's famous folk songs. They have kept alive traditional Latvian music, adding a sense of innovation so that people at home and abroad are always moved and delighted by their music.

Emīls Dārziņš is at the center of this movement, playing a huge role in Latvian classical music by weaving his compositions into the country's folk music heritage. Mr. Dārziņš, both as a pianist and composer, worked hard to join Latvian music and its rhythms with classical music.

Dārziņš' music, a mix of symphonies, chamber music, and choir compositions, not only gained popularity around the world for Latvian folk music but has encouraged new composers in Latvia to fuse classic and contemporary elements. Because of his passion for Latvian traditions and close attention to detail, Dārziņš has made sure the nation's musical scene will not be forgotten for years to come.

Just like Emīls Dārziņš, other Latvian composers have looked to give Latvian folk music a new feel by blending classics from the past with creative modern techniques. The contribution of Jānis Ivanovs and Pēteris Vasks has made sure that Latvian folk music continues to be a valuable part of the nation.

This generation of Latvian artists is interested in learning from the culture's folk songs by reimagining them with different tunes and styles. Thanks to Latvia's innovative singer-songwriters and experimental composers, the local music scene has been reinvigorated and widely shared around the globe.

When we recall the thorough history of Latvian folk music and the individuals who have worked so hard to protect and carry it forward, we are amazed by the permanence of their involvement. Such Masters of the Latvian sound have kept the nation's musical traditions alive, whether they are visionary folklorists, talented agrarian singers, choir leaders, or gifted composers.

They have made it their mission to preserve Latvian music and give it a vibrant future, which keeps catching the eyes and ears of people all over the world. The tradition of Latvian folk music lives on today thanks to the detailed preservation of musical memories and the graceful remodeling of the music.

Parallelled thirds have been a basic building block of Latvian folk music since the beginnings of the nation's music tradition. From its earliest beginnings, Latvian folk music's overlapping tunes, usually accompanied by the rich sounds of the kantele or the steady beat of drums and rattles, would have reminded people of the strong connection they had to their environment.

Over time, the folk music of Latvia kept the parallel third as a strong link uniting its various regional and musical styles. In every style, whether celebratory or nostalgic, Latvian compositions are marked by melody lines that delicately follow the third apart and immediately reveal Latvian roots.

In addition to their function in melodies, parallel thirds have greatly influenced the evolution of

Latvian choral music. The smooth, flowing sound of parallel thirds makes it possible for Latvian composers to create arrangements filled with many harmonies that organically unite all the singers.

Apart from the many parallel thirds, another notable trait of Latvian folk music is the use of modal scales in their songs to give the music an ethereal, mysterious atmosphere.

While Western classical tradition usually relies on major and minor scales, Latvian folk songs are mainly built on modal structures that are much more ancient and basic. By having unequal intervals and changing tonality, these scales create a feeling of unchanging nature, rawness, and human spirituality that Latvians have always valued.

Latvian folk music relies heavily on the Dorian, Phrygian, and Mixolydian modes because they give a mysterious, atmospheric backdrop to reflect on the strange powers seen in the world. The Dorian mode is very common in Latvian songs that express feelings of loss and sadness, and the Phrygian mode is usually heard in their sacred and ceremonial tunes.

Besides being a reflection of Latvia's history

and culture, the main musical features of folk music demonstrate the natural musical sound of the Latvian language. The rhythm and distinctive sounds of Latvian language have served as a main inspiration for the country's musicians, and the use of modal scales develops this inspiration further.

These songs are timeless because Latvian folk music and the Latvian language blend so deeply, catching the essence of all ages. Because of the magical harmonies found in these musical structures, such songs touch on the universal feelings that make up the human experience, crossing over all cultures and regions.

The highest expression of Latvian folk music is its choral sound, a collection of complex, harmonious musical works that represent the true spirit of Latvia. On the world's stages as well as in community settings, the Latvian choral tradition demonstrates how the human voice can fascinate and transform any audience.

The complex, interwoven melodies, the use of modal harmony, and the continuous sound of parallel thirds in Latvian choral music show the nation's close ties with the environment and human nature.

With a foundation in folk music, Latvian choral traditions have greatly contributed to keeping the nation's culture alive.

Latvian choral music not only keeps the country's culture alive, but it also highlights the unique abilities of the human voice to last beyond any period and area. Listening to these works can move and uplift people worldwide, as the wonderful, ghost-like harmony they contain resounds deeply with the feelings shared by everyone.

What sets Latvian folk music apart is the

exciting collection of specific qualities, ranging from haunting melodic lines referencing the unpredictable things in nature to complex, timeless harmonic structures.

Since globalization and the disappearance of cultural traditions are ongoing issues, it becomes even more important that Latvian musical artifacts are present internationally to honor and protect the distinct qualities of music in various cultures. The special harmonies and woven melodies of Latvian folk music are listened to and understood by people of all ages and places.

The unique sounds in Latvian folk music show

how culture can survive and change over time. For countless generations, musicians, choral singers, and composers have worked hard to ensure the unique character of Latvian music stays alive.

Looking at the lasting influence of Latvian musical characteristics, we see that the most interesting and memorable creative works are often connected to people's cultural roots. When we notice these unique music traits, we see how the human spirit still finds a powerful way to be expressed worldwide through sound.

INSTRUMENTS

The kokle, coin of the realm among Latvian musical instruments, has held a notable place in the nation's music for hundreds of years. For a long time, the kokle has been valued as a way for Latvians to express their tradition and culture, thanks to its special tone and ability to hint at mysticism and divinity.

Centuries ago, the kokle, a kind of zither

plucked with fingers, was introduced to Latin traditional music. Made from wood and usually triangular, the kokle is played by plucking its string to create a characteristic rich and haunting sound that is important in Latvian music.

The history of the kokle is full of mystery, as scholars explain that it arose from the long-lasting interaction of ancient Finno-Ugric and Baltic music with Latvian culture. Some suggest that there might be a connection between the kokle and the neighboring kantele, showing that the storied linking of cultures has heavily influenced music in the Baltic states.

Yet, the importance of the kokle goes well past what it looks like or when it first appeared; instead, it represents a purely Latvian spirit and brings its sacred connection to nature and the heavens to life.

So, the way the kokle has always been connected to religion and to the supernatural has created a nearly mythical role for it within Latvian culture.

The presence of the kokle in Latvian music proves that it is an instrument of lasting value and meaningful modifications within the nation's cultural heritage. Since ancient times, when the kokle was a must-have instrument for performing ritual songs, to present-day where it is used in various music forms, the instrument has still a firm and fascinating place in Latvian music.

It is impressive that the kokle has played a big role in saving and carrying forward the ancient songs and poems of the Latvian people. This connection has earned the kokle a large place in the country's music.

With excellent playing, these special tunes bring out the emotional depth hidden in their poetic beauty, making the music very touching.

In both standard folk songs and recent mixes of different genres, the kokle has continued to play a leading role, joining the past and present sounds of music.

Its influence is not limited to saving folk songs in Latvia. Kokles have greatly affected the nation's choral history, lending these songs an air of mysticism that has come to define what people recognize as Latvian music. These feelings and the unique sense of communication with the divine emerge when we listen to the influence of kokle and polyphonic singing.

People who have spent their lives building and preserving kokles are a vital part of why the instrument persists in Latvian music. Thanks to their efforts, the kokle is still around and also carries a strong connection to culture and how individuals sing of their lives.

Because of its original shape and tightly stretched strings, playing the kokle becomes a job of great skill and musical creativity. Every step in a Latvian kokles' construction includes respect for its historic roots and a firm grasp of the unique sounds associated with Latvian music.

While they make the kokle, the makers also keep the tradition alive by handing it down to young people over time. With their careful work and deep knowledge of kokles from different regions, they have guaranteed that this instrument is still alive and significant in Latvian culture.

It's clear from their work that people have always used creativity and strong links between materials, music, and culture. What makes the kokle special is that, besides being a musical instrument, it also represents the Latvian spirit and is the result of generations of effort and dedication from those who build them.

____

Throughout Latvia's musical development and new international influences, the kokle has kept its special place and fits easily into many different modern styles of music.

Renowned Latvian composers have used the kokle's mystical sound in many orchestral and chamberpieces. Most of these pieces, combining the clear tones of the kokle with the colorful performance of Latvian choirs and instrumentalists, have the ability to bring out strong emotions in the listener and show the special and lasting soul of Latvian culture.

Thanks to its special tone and important

____

cultural meaning, the kokle has influenced many contemporary Latvian musicians and composers. With its appearance in both folk and electronic/avant-garde styles, the kokle now plays a big role in supporting the nation's modern music scene with roots and appeal for all listeners.

By pursuing creative, multigenre projects, the kokle has become a key feature of Latvian music and spreads Latvian sounds to people across borders. The ability of a musical instrument to leap over language and cultural differences has helped it sustain itself in the world of music to this day.

When we think about how the kokle shapes Latvian music, we see how it clearly reflects the unique cultural heritage of the country. The kokle's journey started with it being used in rituals to the ancient gods and celebrating the land's changes, and today it is important for carrying on Latvian music traditions.

Even so, its lasting effects include more than its existence and background; it demonstrates how human imagination can cross barriers and help unite many cultures. The amazing sounds of the kokle provide a clear and powerful expression of human life that can move music lovers young and old, no matter where they are.

Deep in the foundation of Latvian instrumental music is a strong respect for the main, intense rhythms tied to the deep importance Latvians attach to nature. The taure and the dūdas are key examples of Latvian folk music, as these wind instruments have greatly influenced the sound of the region.

With its special conical form, the taure, a wood trumpet from Latvia, illustrates the people's deep bond with the natural rhythms. Taure has a deep, excited tone made by vibrating the lips on its narrow opening and gives Latvian folk music a sense of original power and mystery.

It is clear that the honouring of the natural world and appreciation of the land's routine cycles has been part of Argentine culture for a long time. By playing powerful, moving tones, the taure often helped draw attention from the pagan deities responsible for changing the weather and seasons, so the performances were seen as very sacred by the locals.

In addition to the taure, dūdas, Latvian bagpipes, have greatly influenced how Latvian folk music is built rhythmically and harmonically. Their unique drone and ability to make a deep chord have always been related to the joy of new seasons and major

---

agricultural events.

The unique sound of Latvian dūdas, a combination of a filled leather bag and a double reed, often sends listeners back to nature and reminds them of the strong bond that Latvians have always had with the environment. Whether in dance tunes or slower ritual songs, dūdas have always been present in Latvia's music, helping the country's identity reach the audience through sound.

People have always related taure and dūdas to the strong, energetic beats in Latvian folk, yet the country's musical tradition is also known for its elegant melodies, infused with an otherworldly touch—this special quality has become a sign of Latvia's music style.

Stabule, a special type of Latvian flute, is known for helping musicians play the usual haunting melodies common in the country's folk songs. Made from wood and designed so the player can blow at one end, the stabule's tone is soft and heartfelt, inviting the audience to experience powerful emotions that suggest the main elements of nature.

The stabule is strongly linked to Latvian folk music because its magical melodies have often been used to express the nation's strong respect for nature and for the mysteries we encounter in life. Regardless of whether a tune is meant for fans on the dance floor or religious rituals, stabule always stands out in Latvian music, bringing its soothing and lasting sound to the music.

Just like the stabule, the vijole fiddle has made an important contribution to the melodies of Latvian folk music. Because of its unique musical voice and complex melody, the vijole has for a long time expressed the deep link between the Latvians and the spiritual universe.

In the old folk songs from Latvia, the eerie, ghost-like sound of the vijole was meant to express the existence of the pagan divinities who influenced the rhythms of nature. Thanks to the wide range and vibrato-filled melodies produced by the instrument, Latvian musicians can express the essence of human emotion through their songs, making the nation's folk music meaningful to countless people.

In both the lyrical charm of the stabule and the haunting melodies of the vijole, these Latvian musical traditions have strongly influenced the creative side of the nation as they resonate with the Latvian people's close ties to nature and the unknown.

All of these instruments, the taure, the dūdas, the stabule, and the vijole – as important as they are in shaping Latvian music – pale in comparison with a special look at the unique role played by the kokle and the kantele in expressing what it means to be Latvian.

These Latvian instrumental traditions continue to matter because they represent the lasting effects of human creativity on human connections and many traditions. We discover deeply expressive and appealing qualities in the remarkable harmonics of traditional instruments, showing a true artistic image of Latvia.

We discover that the sonic expressions of a small Baltic nation are, in fact, expressions that people everywhere can relate to. Thanks to their unique traits and cultural value, these instruments help unite people and remind us how close we are, apart from our differences.

RESONANCE OF THE PAST

Long celebratory tunes have accompanied Latvian marker moments, just as solemn, quiet music has framed the country's handling of death and mourning, helping the people share their true feelings and most cherished beliefs.

Both when people are enjoying a lively wedding celebration with music and during the bittersweet funeral rites to say goodbye, the

Latvian musical tradition has helped people recognize the importance of meaningful and powerful rhythms in their lives. Not just the sounds of diverse musical styles, but the real feel of Latvia is found in the soft tunes of the kokle, the heavy rhythms of the taure, and the flowing melodies of the stabule.

The makeup of this musical declaration of love and union revolves around the dainas, the famous short poems of Latvian folk music. With their colorful pictures and wonderful metaphors, these poems have given a lot of wedding-themed works their universal touch, showing how human love never changes.

--

The dainas have generally been an integral part of traditional Latvian wedding ceremonies in the past; couples married before friends and family at events where the couple and guests sang dainas that the poet-composer special for the event. The dainas' melodical, rhythmic, and harmonic aspects function as the basis for a surprisingly broad spectrum of musical forms, from bridal processionals to dance tunes for feasting and merrymaking, to lyrical music for facts associated with the solemn vows of meeting as husband and wife, and more.

Even though music and audio aspects of songs are only one part of the wedding, Latvian weddings presented instrumental traditions, not just folk songs or folksongs. The kokle, which is a type of zither with haunting, ethereal tones used in folk-songs, the taure, which is a type of horn used in songs with pulsing, percussive rhythms and the stabule, which is a type of flute used in songs with lyrical, mesmerizing melodies.

However, the Latvian endeavor of mourning and memorialization of individuals transcends primarily the reading of these poetic texts, the son's instrumental traditions play an important role in establishing the soundscape of the funeral. The kokle, for example, produces a haunting and ethereal sound that has been used historically both to honour the dead and give contemplation to the afterlife; its harp-like sonority creates an atmosphere of solemnity and respect.

In concert with the kokle, the Latvian choral tradition has also been an important part of Latvian funerals, with the singing—usually as a group—empowering people to ascend to another level of grief and communal mourning that cannot be replicated by just saying words. The aforementioned dainas are typically used as the source of the texts to these choral works, providing a depth of images and metaphor that are timeless and universal to the fleshy musings of the dearly departed.

The Latvian musical tradition has functioned not only as a conduit of remembrance for the deceased but has also served as an important mechanism wherein humans have wrestled with the deep mysteries of death and dying. The tuneful, mournful branches of Latvian song, the rhythmic, percussive beats, and the distinctive blending of voice and instrument created a sonic experience that connects the human experience of death to cultural identity and universal experience of the most serious of concerns—death and the divine.

More broadly, throughout the events of Latvians rituals and ceremonial life, there has been an enduring and special relationship with nature as well as the cycle of nature and how the seasons enable life and death to co-exist. Latvian music offers sound from joyful, celebratory work songs announcing the beginning of spring to funerary songs that solemnly abandon those moments of autumn that linger before death while reminding listeners of the continuity between heaven and earth. The totality of this Latvian musical lens offers a deep experience of defining the relationship with the sacred.

These seasonal celebrations stem from the old celebrations of the pagan gods and supernatural entities that were associated with the patterns of nature and the seasons. For example, the kokle (often called a lyre or harp), has long been associated with summoning these powers of nature, partly because of the soft, resonant, and heavenly sounds that it produces.

But, of course, Latvians do not venerate nature and celebrate the seasons with mere ritual music. Various instrumental traditions in Latvia add to the music of the rituals and change the soundscape of the celebrations. The taure is a naturally occurring sounding device that can produce sharp, rhythmic, pulsing tones. The taure has been one of the instruments that accompany the bright, joyous, dance-induced melodies that became associated with spring.

The thorny, ripped and ripped once coincided with invocation of nature and the blessings that nature provided, from snow melting or grass growing to celebratory spring and summer.

The stabulē's musical, ethereal notes had often been heard accompanying autumn harvest times; their soft, warm-whispering notes conjuring the earth's wealth and plenty and in doing so, indicate how Latvians valued the repeat patterns of nature. Likewise, the rich, polyphony of Latvian choral music has served an important role in these seasonal aspects as well, offering emotive and collective interpretations to how humanness is humbled and understood as part of the divine; to engage in ways that respect their place/connection to the natural world initiates, foster creativity and respect for the relationship ultimately elicits more emotive responses.

With this set of elements the Latvian musical ecology fuses the dreamy, ethereal kokle, the ebbing and flowing breath of the taure as a rhythm, lyrical loveliness that stabulē evokes, rich beauty and harmony generated by choral music, etc. This offers an expression of the Latvian way to respect the natural cycles, as a cycle of celebration acknowledging natural cycles, as evidenced by the ability for music to provide a meaningful engagement space for expressions of sense of place, anthropological cultural group identity, being religious/spiritual, and the psyches of human condition.

In the contexts of the traditional Latvian wedding ceremony, where the dainas, along with the Latvian instrumental repertoire, has constructed exclamatory glimmers in the mediating soundscape of the performance as something transcending the rhythms of the cosmopolitan heart, and the traditional funerary rites, where folk instrumental and song traditions served to remember and venerate those who loss, the musical tradition of Latvia has served as a transitory space where values, beliefs, and cultural norms have been both preserved and reproduced.

But the enduring musical traditions of Latvia went far beyond the ritual and ceremonial contexts in which they were often found. They represent a necessary means to communicate a coherent cultural identity and a sense of belonging for+ the people of Latvia. Whether it was the collective performance of the dainas, the collective participation in the seasonal celebrations, or the collective and emotive ceremonial expressions during the rite of funerals, they all contributed to the musical experience of performance and the soundscape of community and cosmopolitan belonging that transcended space and time and reminded partner and listener of their shared identity and experience in a particular moment, and a Latvian daina, sonorous and often melancholic laments or celebratory songs, remains a cultural touchstone for all Latvians.

The extraordinary ability for flexibility and transformation attests to the inherent power of the Latvian folk music tradition, a living tradition deeply rooted in rhythms and cadences of the Latvian language and of the connections among human beings and nature. Because of the social, political, and cultural contexts of Latvia are constantly changing and fluctuating, the role of folk music has always remained a constant that captures the essence of a timeless legacy of melody, harmony, and rhythm brought to life by the folk musician, the composer, and the cultural bearer.

Latvian folk music's ability to endure in spite of adversity tells a story about the power of human creativity to transcend the almost insurmountable challenges of history. The long geopolitical periods of colonial or foreign rule denying the normal expression of its cultural life as well as the opening and shutting tides of global impact formed powerful foundations and trajectories interacting in ways to create the unique landscape of Latvian music. There have been adjustments and reshaping of the tradition in order to evolve as needed but effectively, the Latvian folk music tradition is an effective, reproducible, and memorable way to connect to and document human history through music, song, and dance.

A powerful image of this resilience lives in the folk music of Latvia, particularly in reaction to the Soviet occupation of the country in the 20th century. Opposed to an intent to erase the cultural identity of the country and incorporate it into the overarching Soviet model, the people of Latvia called on their musical traditions to help preserve their cultural uniqueness and national pride.

The choral tradition of Latvia became a

powerful and a public symbol of this resistance with the multiple, polyphonic harmonies served as a soundscape of the nation. As the Soviet authorities sought to create control and censorship around the traditional folk songs and pastimes, the people of Latvia found ways, creatively, to subvert the approved system by adding fragments of traditional folk music into their compositions that appeared to exist inside the approved cultural constraints.

This incredible agility for adaptation and reinvention would also apply to choral music forms. In the large field of the Latvian folk music tradition, musicians and composers took the ancient sound of the kokle and related it to

---

the contemporary percussion of the taure, allowing them to create ways of mapping sounds of both expressions of Latvian meaning and musical form into one presentation of music, as a collective. They created new compositions that contained cultural and historical meaning for their nation, but could also connect with the contemporary audience's tastes and rapidly changing attitudes as a society.

In the end, all of this meant that the tradition of Latvian folk music not only survived the historical circumstance that initiated the historic appropriation of the art form; it thrived! The ability to reinterpret and preserve these

---

centuries-old melodies, rhythms, and harmonies became part of their resistance and identity as a nation, and to actualize and make sense of their place within human creativity.

The journey of Latvian folk music goes much further than recreating the poetic lyrics. Highly trained instrumentalists and vocalists find new ways to revitalize the old musical forms and context that have dominated the auditory experience of listeners for centuries. The kokle, for example, with its otherworldly timbres, has been integrated into several contemporary genres including highly personal folk inspired performances by singer-songwriters to fully electronic and avant-garde re-interpreted compositions.

Similarly, the vibrant rhythms of the taure and the spinetingling melodies of the stabule are now being revived by Latvian musicians who, through their own creativity, are stretching the bounds of Latvian folk music beyond simply their predecessors expression of it. By merging the identity of these instruments with the aesthetics and methods of contemporary musicians, and capturing an electric vitality in their offering they create an experience vibrant and present for local and global audiences who can engage with their material.

However, the journey of Latvian folk music is not purely an individual artistic voyage; it is focused upon the strength of collective cultural organizations and the hard efforts of people willing to devote their lives toward preserving and sustaining folk music traditions in their country. Latvia has put forth both scholarly and vernacular work at the hands of folklorists and ethnomusicologists, collective community building with folk discourse, and otherwise active performance of traditional songs and navigation of instrument techniques. The Latvian people, as a community, have shaped and reshaped their working definition of the folk music tradition to ensure that the quintessential essence remains a vibrant facet of their cultural domain.

Moreover, the same structures and techniques that have continued the soundscape of this zeitgeist – polyphonic contours, modal harmonies, instrument sound structures – have acted as/value added bridges of access for musicians and composers outside the boundaries of the Baltic state. The incorporation of an authentic Latvian folk element to classical music; the dynamic and hybrid genre (folk, classical, jazz, punk, and experimental) music and art forms performed by some internationally recognized folk ensembles, have expanded the ethnomusicological inquiry into this folk music, carrying forward the influence this music can and has inspired worldwide.

CHORAL TRADITIONS

In Latvia, choral music is important to culture because it is important to the spirit of the culture as a whole, it builds upon rich, polyphonic, expressions of artistic value. It can be heard in either traditional folk song arrangements, or in the diversity of genres explored by many choral ensembles. Throughout the many years of the Latvian choral experience, choral music has been an integral way to transmit and preserve culture, values, beliefs, and artistic expression.

Latvian folk music has been an important part of the choral experience, as evidenced in the incorporation of poetic texts from folk music form to be used as texts. Folk music is also found in the melodic structure, modal harmonies, and polyphonic compositions that have traditionally formed the canon of folk music, and these folk elements have been similarly integrated into the choral repertoire and artistic expression, uniquely and powerfully tied to the Latvian cultural identity, as well as the creative musical experience for the audience.

The kokle, a plucked zither-like instrument now an icon of Latvian music history, has had an important role in the choral tradition. The kokle's haunting, airy tones probably provided, and continue to provide, a unique and valuable aspect of choral compositions and accompaniment. It's harp-like quality provided a sacred and mystical aspect of the Latvian choral tradition, intimately connecting these sounds to our pagan past and the rhythm of nature.

The association of these tonal, modal harmonies and polyphonic textures of the dainas with the kokle's resonant sounds has embedded the choral tradition strongly to

Latvian culture, both musically and physically, in ways that are true to the traditions of the past, but at the same time fresh and present – the music embodies both the heritage and cultural evolution of a people.

Folk music/music of the nation, as part of the cultural context of the nation, and collaterally, specifically the choral tradition/Choral music of the nation has preserved, sustained, and propagated the cultural heritage of the nation – basic values, beliefs, and expression – throughout time.

Latvia has a large historical base of musical

traditions, including one of the most significantly rich choral traditions in the world. It is not the rich, polyphonic harmonies contained within much of the Latvian choral repertoire that captures the country's deep association with nature and its mysterious processes and cycles. It is the ethereal and haunting characteristics of many of these choral works that connected to the spirituality of the human experience, supporting modal harmonies, interlacing strands of melody, allowing us to think more deeply about what "the elements", "the primal", "the totally spiritual" each as components connected to a bigger piece of Latvia's identity. Our means of understanding the spiritual and natural worldview provided us with a rich lens of understanding and creating those common ties.

However, the weight of the choral tradition as an expression of cultural heritage moves much further beyond purely musical articulation of Latvia's spiritual and naturalist perspectives. The sounds of Latvia have served as meaningful means of reconciliation and veneration of the spirit of Latvia's people, their common history and experiences of being vulnerable, and their tenacious quest for cultural independence in anti-pravantujoti-particularly-Iron Curtain nations, which sought to eradicate their autonomy and cultural identity over centuries of original movement.

The Latvian Song and Dance Festivals, for example, have evolved into an iconic, cherished, and critical part of who Latvians are as a nation. They celebrate the resilience of the Latvian people while providing a huge opportunity for massive groups of choirs and members of the public to congregate. These major celebrations are communal celebrations of large choral and dance ensembles of multi-part choral works and choreographed dance that witness the ongoing expression of the Latvian national identity. The festivals showcase the adaptation and trends in Latvian choral compositions, alongside the Latvian cultural legacy to provide laments to, and rich spectacles to, memorialize and bind the experience of the traditional choral form in a both evocative soundscapes and colorful, physical movement.

The Latvian choral tradition continues to be preserved, developed, and promoted by conductors, composers, and cultural guardians who are committed to fulfilling purpose from the nation's rich history and continue to excel, and insist on adapting new variables within the choral tradition, while maintaining the values of one of the country's most basic artistic cultural traditions. It is both within the vibrant setting of the international Song and Dance Festivals or through the intimate offerings of the smaller, community based choral ensembles that proliferate throughout Latvia that have made

---

this a significant form of sound practice to transmit the Latvian experience and legacy from the past to the present, and the future. It is likely to continue doing so for generations to come.

The spiritual significance of the Latvian choral tradition is much greater than a simple presence of elements of traditional folk music and folk instrumental performance practice. The same forms and stylistic sensibilities that have autthenticated this musical inheritance – the rich polyphony, the modal harmonies, the hauntingly beautiful melodies – have become sacred, opportunities to realize potentials at the edge of the human condition.

The choral performances often take on a quasi-religious purpose, as the huge, community activities have recognized the Latvian spirit and the ongoing relationships among the Latvian people and with the mysteries of what lies beyond our physical reality. The force and emotional impact of the choral events can elevate a listener to a place or contemplation that enables a sense of the universal, the eternal, and the sacred.

In both large, public gatherings such as the Song and Dance Festivals, and smaller, localized community-based choral groups, these diverse voice forms have unified people together from many identities and experiences to proclaim the life force of the nation.

As we think about the depth and complexity of meaning of the Latvian choral tradition, we are inevitably excited by the potency of indigenous choral expression, and its ability to mesmerize, invigorate, and unify a community, both within the defined borders of the Baltic nation and across the globe. From the large, impassioned compositions of choral works staged within major international concert halls, to smaller, community-based ensembles, preserving local practical music making traditions, the Latvian choral tradition has and will continue to play an essential and indispensable part of the culture of their country, preserving the voices of the

___

Latvian community with sonic representations of their collective identity, faith, and connection to the extended rhythms of humanity.

The National Song and Dance Festival is by far the most important Latvian national expression. A large congregation and public gathering which has captivated the Latvian people for over a century, this enormous event demonstrates the power of song and dance to create a collective identity, preserve a heritage and instill cultural pride in the people.

The first Latvian National Song and Dance Festival began as an idea in the mid-19th century, an important time for the nation of Latvia which was marked by the development of national and cultural awakening. In a time of increased political and social turmoil, several Latvian intellectuals and cultural advocates started the Riga Latvian Society that sought to uphold and promote the artistic and folkloric traditions of the nation.

In this context the first Latvian National Song Festival took place in 1873. The festival was a small event of choirs and folk musicians, but one that proclaimed the resolve of the Latvian people to assert their cultural identity with mounting political and social repression. In the years that followed, the festival travelled to larger venues with more and more performers and audiences, adding to the festival's significance as a focal point in the nation's struggle for independence and self-determination.

But with the emergence of dance at the festival in the early 20th century, the festival's relevance grew substantially. The dynamic, choreographed fun routines provided a way to announce the Latvian people's rootedness in the land amidst the rhythms of the world. This addition of dance forged a powerful connection between song and dance, voice and body, would be constitute a latent characteristic of the Latvian National Song and Dance Festival, enveloping the festival in a universe of total expression that was inescapable for audience members and performers alike.

Despite the upheavals and occupations that Latvia endured throughout the events of 20th century, the Song and Dance Festival always represented a constant, sustaining cultural event in the Latvian identity. Even through the darkest days of Soviet occupation, it continued to be a symbol of and a vessel through which the most important artistic and spiritual traditions continued to exist.

Since Latvia's independence was restored in

1991, the Song and Dance Festival has continued to evolve, adopting new musical and choreographic practices, but staying committed to paying tribute to, and celebrating, Latvia's rich cultural legacy. Today, the event represents the ability of shared artistic expression as a form of communion across time and space, and the festival continues to attract the interest of the public both locally within Latvia and afar, outside of the Baltic state.

It would be difficult to overstate the significance of the Latvian National Song and Dance Festival. As a large-scale, community-wide celebration of cultural anchoring, the event brought together a collective identity, retained a collective tradition, and fostered a remarkable collective pride of culture in the Latvian experience.

The festival's relevance is much more than the actual performance of these art forms. Rather, it is a necessary mode of transferring the nation's cultural heritage from generation to generation, thus preserving the fundamental values, beliefs and traditions that form the basis of the Latvian experience. The continuity and relevance of Latvian cultural norms will carry on and resonate with the future generations.

By the nature of the festival's ambience, the celebratory form is collective, so there is a shared experience among performers and audiences alike through their contribution to an active communal cultural expression. The Song and Dance Festival is an effective tool for cross-pollinating cultural consciousness; an experience through honor and individual culture, collective shared experiences through song dance and artistic expression preserve identification and sense of belonging in many ways as it connects the experiencing citizens of Latvia and beyond.

The expressive implications of the Latvian National Song and Dance Festival are endless.

It is an effective cultural ambassador that goes beyond the constraints of a Baltic state and can drive audiences around the world crazy with excitement. The dimensions of the festival are epic in proportion, and the whole performance itself kind of envelopes you in different geo-political and historically influenced ways. It is so relatable and applicable as an artistic expression. The choral and dance performance is full of inherent emotion, breath and space that transcends uniqueness of place and event but still maintains eloquent and effortless distinctiveness as an expression of cultural identity.

In the years since the restoration of

independence in Latvia, the Song and Dance Festival has developed and transformed, bringing forth new musical and choreography while continuing to respect and honour their history and importance to the culture. And, thanks to the hard work of talented conductors, choreographers, cultural guardians, these globalized festivals have acted as a community tool affirming the identity and hope of the Latvian people, giving powerful resonance to their creative capacity as social beings throughout the country and beyond.

Despite the ongoing significance of the Latvian National Song and Dance Festival, it should be noted that today's choral music from Latvia has also gained an important international profile, with Latvian choirs and conductors at times dominating prestigious festivals and competitions around the world.

One prime example is the World Choir Games, which is now a biennial event with the reputation of the Olympics of the choral world, attracting choirs from over 70 countries to gather, compete and create in a spectacle of celebration of the human voice and choral singing. The Latvian choir tradition differentiates itself at this competition by their richly, and beautifully, woven polyphonic harmonies, the often hauntingly poetic celestial tones, and creative commitments to presenting both everyday, traditional, and contemporary repertoire. They have wowed large audiences, and jury members, at the World Choir Games since the inaugural World Choir Games in 2000 in Germany.

Still, the international influence of Latvian choral music is not solely related to its competitive context; national ensembles and conductors have also played a significant role in the well-known Riga Jurmala Music Festival, an annual festival of some of the best classical musicians and ensembles in the world, where Latvian choral music and artistry merits a place in the festival with the programming regularly including the beautiful, virtuosic performances of Latvian vocal ensembles.

The global resonance and influence of the Latvian choral tradition has a multitude of reasons and probably due to many factors, and not the least of which is the very real connection these aural expressions have to the cultural roots of the nation as well. The influence of the dainas, the poetic treasures that have served as the lyrical inspiration for Latvian folk music, are arguably evident within the modal and at times haunting harmonies and interwoven melodic lines connected to the Latvian choral pieces.

The worldwide impact of the Latvian choral tradition also reflects the incredible artistry and technical finesse of these choirs and conductors and their ongoing mastery of the expressive and emotive power of the human voice. Whether these choral performances were part of the large, public, and community events at the World Choir Games, or part of more intimate and chamber-based events at the Riga Jurmala Music Festival, these Latvian singers have an ability to wow and enthrall audiences with a timeless, universal quality to their sound.

As the Latvian nation moves forward in the currents of the modern age, the continued

---

presentations of its choral traditions at festivals around the world have been a critical way for Latvia to assert cultural sovereignty and share its artistic heritage and identity with the world. Through the continuing work of conductors, composers, and cultural custodians, these expressive sounds have continued to change, evolve, and grow to combine ancient traditions with contemporary themes and ideas while still representing a commitment to the essence of the Latvian voice.

By sharing a word, song, and dance line that resides in traditions and repertoires of the past, sting with poetics from the traditions of folk music and then liberating them from that trinity of traditional forms, made it possible for the timeless music and rhythm of pieces engrained in the Latvian folk music tradition, the modern sounding mash-ups can still deliver this sound and sight, all while maintaining the ever-changing, ever-evolving, vitality that has moved beyond any boundaries or perceived confines.

CLASSICAL MUSIC

Classical music has historically stood eminent and fascinatingly positioned as the very organ through which the nation's artistic heritage has been conserved into being, and at the same time, straining for creative innovation. Anything from large, grand, dramatic symphonic works which form, in many respects, the core of the Latvian orchestral repertoire to the more delicate and nuanced operatic and concert stage works-well, the tradition of Latvian classical music has, through ages, known to very well adapt and recreate itself, proving itself able to marry the classical elements of the bygone era with the practical needs and the creative energies of a contemporary day.

There has been placed consideration behind the ancient respect musicians have had for the rich and varied musical traditions which are part of the Latvian cultural landscape. The haunting and mystical tones of Latvian folk tunes, the different moods created by the numerous polyphonic structures of choral music, the mysterious modal sonic atmospheres so strong to become brand identity of Latvia- all these have greatly inspired and provided doors of expression to the Latvian composers that have been cultivating the genre of classical music through the rites of their lives.

Latvia's classical tradition means far more than just the integration of exclusive musical materials into the art. It stands for a deep and lasting commitment toward protecting and developing this artistic form, for successive generations of Latvian composers and musicians have toiled under oftentimes immense hardship to ensure that Latvian cultural heritage is not only preserved but continually reimagined and interpreted for the present day.

Under the aegis of such artists and protectors of culture, Latvian classical music tradition has become a sound tapestry, knitting together different strings of the nation's musical past and present into one great harmonious whole that has been and still remains an inspiring and transformative force for audiences worldwide.

The ensemble of eminent composers and conductors has made their vast personal and creative contributions to the adornment of the Latvian classical tradition while also securing the nation's reputation abroad.

Elements forming the core of the Latvian orchestral repertoire and which represent Emīls Dārziņš as a towering figure included mostly his works. Dārziņš, the virtuoso pianist and gifted melodist, bestowed upon the Latvian classics a large and largely symphonic body of works which integrate the elements of Latvian folk music into the common classical language, thus rendering a symphonic treatment to the sacred concept of timelessness in these sounds.

Form and harmony were exerted by Ēriks Dārziņš in his compositions, imparting upon them a rather specific expression of culture and yet a universal message, so to say; in the fusion were the eerie, almost ecstatic melodies, and modal harmonies of Latvian folk tradition with vast, lyrical gestures of the Romantic symphonic tradition. His so-called "Suites" and "Tone Poems" are perhaps the most cherished concert pieces in the Latvian concert halls, touching the hearts of many that feel they sing the very essence of the nation's cultural identity.

Dārziņš was not alone in leaving a mark on the panorama of Latvian classical music. Alongside Ēriks Dārziņš stood Jānis Mediņš, a master of thickly orchestrated, harmonically complex works that drew at times deeply upon the choral tradition of the country, and Jānis

Ivanovs, who proceeded to fuse rhythmical and melodic idioms from traditional Latvian folk music with vigorous genre-wide composition.

Together with their contemporaries, these composers were forging an outright Latvian classical music tradition-rooted in the country's rich cultural framework but pushing the boundaries of creative expression. With threads pulled together from the woven fabric of the Latvian sonic tapestry-folk melodies, choral harmonies, and modal inflections-they would build a symphonic repertory that could enthrall audiences both at home and across the oceans as dire ambassadors of the artistic heritage of their country.

Next to this shining tradition of Latvian classical music is the country's opera and ballet repertoire that has contributed towards the contours of the country's culture; allowing the opportunity to showcase the Latvian cultural legacy at its most valid and exciting.

Margeris Zariņš An unquestioned master of dramatic narrative and musical characterisation, Margeris Zariņš drew on Latvia's rich myth and folk traditions to produce operas and ballets that distil eternal features of the Latvian cultural heritage into the dynamic and emotive gestures of the lyric theatre. The prescient works of Zariņš have gone on to define the Latvian stage.

One of Zariņš' most acclaimed compositions, the opera "Fires of Kurzeme", showcases how this composer could integrate and unite the various threads of Latvian art in a single performance. The tale of a the desperate and violent struggle between Latvian partisans and invading German forces, it borrows from the nation's rich history and mythology and ensures a sense of sweeping, cinematic grandeur that is equaled only by the profound emotional impact of the work.

Yet, whereas the composer had an immense

impact on Latvian operatic and ballet tradition, the nature of his influence was such that he would have extended so much more in assistance to the performers. He was a subject-so-respected instructor and mentor who assisted many tutoring Latvian composers and prepared them. Thus, they are able to create a healthy and active panorama for performances that invite attention and audience in both stages of the country and exterior.

Alongside Zariņš, other Latvian composers have also deeply impacted the lyric theatre tradition of the country. Artists like Artūrs Maskats and Ēriks Ešenvalds write operas and ballets that blend strong dramatic elements and passionate harmonies of the Western canon with the unique elements of music that have, since times immemorial, defined Latvian artistic identity.

Owing to the unrelenting efforts from these artists, the Latvian operatic and ballet repertory have come to be perceived as an established and revered part of the cultural fabric of the nation, lifting the Latvian artistic legacy to new and exciting heights. These musical and visual arts are capable of producing grandiose, sweeping productions for the stages of the best operas in the country or a small, intimate chamber piece that converses with intricate varieties of the human condition.

As the Latvian classical music tradition developed and matured through the 20th and 21st centuries, composers and performers of the country have exerted very deep and lasting influences over the world stage, thus fascinating audiences, critics, and peers.

Among the principal giants of Latvian classical music crowned with international fame is Mariss Jansons, conductor and composer. A veritable interpreter of orchestral repertoire, Janson is richly lauded for his vivid, heartfelt performances of both the Latvian symphonic repertoire and that of the Western tradition in repute worldwide; through his interpretations, he bears the distinctive musical character of his Baltic homeland.

However, Jansons is not the only Latvian classical artist whose works have been appreciated on the world stage. The pianist Vestards Šimkus, famous for his electroshock style performances throughout New York and Tokyo, and the violinist Baiba Skride, known for the Latvian violin concertos, have also played a huge role in giving the Latvian musical experience visibility.

The movements of these artists outside of their national identity and into the world stage indicate that there can be a universal and artistic impact from Latvian musicians. They created music through their virtuoso skills and devotion to the cultural traditions of Latvia. When they perform music, they connect to the shared human experience with genre specificity and indescribable emotion.

Latvian classical music has a worldwide impact well outside individual artists and performers. Indeed, composers in Latvia have influenced the world in a deep and lasting way, as composers like Emīls Dārziņš, Jānis Mediņš, and Ēriks Ešenvalds have received tremendous critical success and applause from orchestras, opera companies, and chamber ensembles around the world.

CONTEMPORARY VOICES

Latvian musical expression today is very much a blend of past folk tradition and the contemporary genre-crossing developments being produced by a new generation of creators. It encompasses everything from singer-songwriters drawing on folk and soul traditions to contemporary electronic and avant-garde composers. It can also be said that all of these contemporary Latvian voices are taken together, masterful storytellers expressing their creativity within the timeless melody and rhythm encapsulated in Latvian folk music and drawing on Latvia's unique cultural identity.

While unique to Latvian music, the lyrical references and Morse themes offer rich source material for story queries that can be shared and are universal. They take the reader through a branch of evocative imagery and metaphor and many years of a prior and more timely context while allowing for a complete absorption of traditional and contemporary.

The importance of these new Latvian interpreters of folk tradition goes far beyond a reanimation of a musical tradition. They are taking traditional songs and tradition and not only revitalizing the soundscapes but also creating new hybrid fusions that introduce haunting, timeless melodies and modal harmonies into semi-structured performances that astonish and transform audiences, both inside and beyond the boundaries of the Baltic state.

Whether it is the artistry of singer-songwriters such as Kārlis Auzāns, who weave their emotions, fierce vocals and guitars into the essence of the Latvian spirit in their folk-inspired music, or the bravado of artists such as Reinis Sējāns, who produce experimental electronic pieces as a blend of his sonic worlds and also meld with the primordial rhythms of the world around him, these new Latvian folk-inspired voices have opened the boundaries of what passion-driven Latvians now consider their folk musical identity.

Along with the burgeoning singer-songwriter movement influenced by folk, the Latvian contemporary music scene has also been enlivened by the growing number of rock and metal bands that blend the past and use their own stylistic vision to add the wealth of the nation's traditional music to their evolving generational representation.

At the forefront of this sonic revolution stands acclaimed metal act Skyforger, whose sweeping, symphonic works influence by modal harmonies, with their haunting melodies, and throbbing rhythms that evoked the feel of Latvian folk music forms, instrumental mastery, and respect for the nation's cultural depth, produces a sonic experience that is rooted in the unchanging traditions and folklore of the past, while capturing the raw sensations present in contemporary sensory surroundings.

Skyforger is not the only band rooted in Latvian rock and metal that are mixing folk-element roots with contemporary sounds. Līvi, with their more folk-sounding heavy metal infused approach, Dzelzs Vilks, with its more atmospheric, progressive forms of music mixing the elemental rhythms rooted in Latvian lore and traditions have each contributed to the redefinition of the sonic found in experiences of Latvia's cultural identity, creating a completely new blend of past and contemporary sounds.

The unique feature of these Latvian rock and metal bands is not only their technical proficiency or their mastery in creating catchy, cross-genre tunes. The defining feature is the commitment to engage with the nation's cultural heritage; integrating folk melodies, instruments, and lyrical themes into their music is surely the most meaningful way they create culturally specific and therefore universal sound.

When rock and metal artists use an instrument with cultural specificity like the kokle, a plucked instrument akin to zither that has become associated with Latvia, and/or when they infuse their lyrics with the meta- and imagistic traditions of dainas, they show an ability to engage with their culture and create a new sound that combines the best elements of their folk legacy with the best elements of their shared rock and metal cultures.

Kristaps Krievkalns, an exceptional pianist and

composer, is at the forefront of this exciting blend of styles, presenting attractive compositions that have received a great deal of critical acclaim, in Latvia and around the globe. Krievkalns is remarkable in his integration of distinctly Latvian folk characteristics - melancholic, modal harmonies, lyrical, meandering melodies, pulsing, percussive rhythms, along with the virtuoso improvisational character of jazz tradition - into a musical soundscape that is rooted in the imagery of Latvia, but speaks with an innovative creative voice.

The Rūta Dūduma Quartet, whose vibrant, integrating interpretations of Latvian folk songs have developed a dedicated following both at home and internationally, and the Tērbatas Kvartets, whose tranquil and spirit-oriented compositions emphasize the elemental, mystical spirit of rhythmic motifs in the Latvian land; all demonstrate a vibrant element of innovation that has produced a new and engaging synthesis of musical yesterdays with contemporary practices.

What makes the Latvian jazz scene unique is not only its musical artistry and complex sound, but also the way these artists treat this work with honor and respect for the rich tapestry of Latvian culture and history. It isn't just meant to represent the people of Latvia, but to capture the heritage of the country through updated folk songs, sounds of folk or traditional instruments, and even imbedded folk rhythms. The Latvian jazz scene, like our nation, is a merger of the past with the modern, recreating and remixing, imagining new ways to create and invoke the peoples' cultural identity through sound. Audiences from Latvia and around the world have been inspired and are interpreting musical histories from Latvia in different and crucially important ways.

Of course, this hybrid scene is celebrating and experiencing the development of a new generation of electronic musicians and avant-garde artists. The contemporary music scene in

---

Latvia is expanding and developing, presenting new work and re-imagining previous relationships with Latvian sound from the past. These contemporaries are working with sound histories from Latvia using new technology and creative approaches to composition.

An established composer and auditory artist, Reinis Sējāns is particularly interested in this generation. Sējāns began gaining notoriety for experimental work in Latvia and beyond. Sējāns seems interested in possessing the essence of the low, primal sounds and rhythm's vital space within the estuary of life.

Sējāns's creative imagination goes beyond just reproducing natural sounds or rhythms. Sometimes his works act to effectively consolidate the modal harmonies, lyrical melodies, and unique instrumental timbres that have existed in Latvian folk music for centuries into a lively and genre-mixed musical fabric that respects traditional cultural forms while engaging with cutting-edge electronic music.

Sējāns is not the only Latvian electronic musician who has achieved such potential with regard to electronic music's relationship to tradition. Other musicians like Kārlis Auzāns, who often provided fascinating and genre-bending compositions that combine folk, ambient, and electronic influences, as well as Dārta Jansone, whose atmospheric and reflective sound often seeks to evoke the mystical patterns of the Latvian natural landscape, make a contribution to the greater task of continuing to develop and articulate the evolving identity of Latvian music, drawing equally from significant elements of the past and inspiring visions of the future.

What is interesting about Latvian electronic music is the palpable sense of deep cultural identity and global relevance that these formally experimental sounds project. They have been able to connect to the very being of Latvianness, about creating a vibrant and unusual sound not only connects with audiences differently but captures and transmogrifies audiences in every space. Be it through ethereal, uncanny layers displaying the rhythms of the natural order, or the usage of both traditional folk instrumentation and melodies freely interlaced with processes, assemblage, and new creation. The same can be said for a new generation of creative musicians, both in folk and singer-songwriter tradition, who have a strong sense of roots but are killing it in the new space.

For example, for a new generation of female singer-songwriters such as Rozenes, Patrimonio or Zante, who are digging deep into folk influences in a soulful fashion. Or through new gendered roles of musical activity enabled through local experimentations or worlds of complex new age compositors, artists like Ieva Bormane and Krišjānis Stabulnieks are able to speak about different forms of Latvia merchant class avant-garde traditions, using past to think anew, all without abandoning knowing and belonging to home, like selfless true home regions, such as a Latvian *ןש* where yamaka in part shared provides artist stage to the sorts of edges discussed above. Different forms of contemporary responses used as pathways to prove Latvianness in currently explored doubts of global contemporary countries retaining borders.

It is remarkable how the new voices from Latvia have been shaping and captivating audiences across the globe. The folk-inspired singer-songwriters, the orchestral symphonic music and soundscapes of rock and metal bands, the experimental sonic interpretations of jazz musicians, and, no doubt, the extraordinary reach of their experimental electronic soundscapes have added a bold new chapter to the ongoing saga of how Latvian music identifies and expresses cultural identity's endless continuation, all the while paying homage to Latvia's rich cultural history.

This phenomenal global reach of Latvian

sounds has allowed the world to experience its unique sounds through a somewhat un-planned series of 21st century phenomena, each one playing a key component in the nation's ability to share its talented artistic history, its culture, and its rich heritage with the world. Undoubtedly, the rise of digital technologies, the broadening scope of international cultural exchange projects, and the incessant work of musicians, composers, and custodians of culture have initiated a continual movement of Latvian sonic expressions, so that the genuine sonic print that local talents have made in notion of Latvian ontology continues to speak to numerous audiences well beyond the borders of the Baltic state.

The global significance of Latvian music is more than just a question of commerciality and prestige. It is about the universality and transformative properties of these sound expressions, with the potential to connect, to foster understanding and to nurture reaffirmation of our sameness as humans. In whatever form it presents, such as the powerful crowning choral compositions of the nation, the contemporary pieces that stitch together past and future, and the contemporary collaborations that weave genres together, Latvian music has proven an amazing capacity to cut through borders of language, culture and geographic contexts, to provoke fundamental issues dealing with the human condition.

Latvian choral music has the potential for global significance due to a number of reasons, not least of which would be the emotional and spiritual resonances these sound expressions have the capacity to evoke. The rich and polyphonic textures of a balanced Latvian choral work, the modal harmonic structures, and the definitionally catchy elemental or melismatic melodies of their canon straddle varied depths of the human experience, and invite some desire for connection with each other, to contemplate deeper, and to reconfirm, to fly into expanses of human separation, to transcend barriers of language and culture, through music.

Latvian choir music has an important responsibility in the world beyond beauty. Latvia's vocal ensembles have also demonstrated phenomenal technical ability and creative imagination, captivating audiences and earning the respect of peers and critics with their passionate, spirited interpretations of both classic and contemporary works. The world has regarded and respected these choral musicians, high-fidelity musicians who interpret musical performance contexts, what they sing, works that underscore the Latvian culture, and own works that blend Latvian musical legacy with new creative practice regardless of whether they perform their legacy works or bold, genre-bending composition.

Helped by the hard work of Latvia's excellent conductors and cultural guardians who have directed their efforts to bring their unique acoustic fingerprints of their history of music to the soundscapes of the world, Latvia's choral tradition has gained worldwide significance. These committed performers have ensured that the buoyant spirit of Latvian choral music has persevered in soundscapes around the world using avenues such as international tours, elite performance at festivals, and creative formats in collaboration with ensembles in other parts of the world. This has cultivated rich relationships that have fostered greater appreciation for the country of Latvia and its rich heritage.

As Latvian music continues to enchant and redefine audiences on international platforms, the impact of these sound expressions is growing clearer; the nation's variety of musical traditions provide a way for them to reach beyond cultures and build bridges with some connector of our shared experience as part of a global family.

These sound expressions seem to transcend languages, cultures and geographies, in terms of the strength that the impact of the Latvian choral tradition to take people into large realms of extreme spiritual and emotional meaning, or consider the thoughts of globalizing contemporary music scene where inventors' of sound might not only create genre bent pieces but bring listeners universal meanings of shared human existence.

The very nature of creative work requires collaborations with others, international festivals and competitions, and the smart use of digital technology, are just a few of the ways that Latvian musicians and cultural gatekeepers have coming together to present the distinct sound print of Latvia's creative memory to the world, drive a stronger interest, and raise the profile of Latvian music to new listeners and institutional partners. These efforts have also intended to help others appreciate and understand Latvian cultural heritage - perhaps inspiring listeners to be in awe, or treat each other with respect and connectedness regardless of their background.

THE CULTURAL TAPESTRY

Latvian music is heavily linked with other art forms in a way that provides a lot of insight into the cultural identity and socio-historical progress of the country. To fully appreciate Latvian music, one must probe its interconnections with other art forms, namely literature, the visual arts, and dance, as well as how these relationships have informed each other historically. What will be discovered is a web of creative activity that is united through common themes, practices, and meaning. By examining these connections, we can examine ways in which the larger narrative of culture is developing through clear, albeit overlapping, domains of expression.

The connectedness of Latvian literary and musical practices is most apparent: these are two of the deepest artistic affinities in Latvian culture. This connection can be traced back millennia to collective sharing of folk poems and rhymes that enlivened by indigenous make-up and music. When written literary traditions developed, poets and playwrights like Rainis which firmly established the works were steeped in vernacular rhymes and rhythms which gave the verses the same musical bounce as songs typically provided. So, it is no surprise that many established utterly writing and lyric partnerships with Latvian composers who set the poems to entirely original compositions and thus enhanced the emotional timbre of the verses.

The work of Rainis discloses underlying inquiries into course markers for Latvian identity and the improvement of society in a discourse with philosophical verse. Rainis' poetic imagery invites the pastoral into his poems that comment existentially on questions of national identity at a stormy hour in history. Composers noted this spirituality and understanding and transmitted these higher. One of Rainis's works, for example, "Pūt, vējiņi!" has become extremely famous, whose choral work by Viesturs Skujenieks exquisitely captured the melancholy beauty and patriotic spirit of the poem. Rainis delved into music, sharing with others his message embodied in the lyrics, while the composers saw in these verses their own themes to elaborate on in new forms of music.

This collaboration survives beyond the lifetime of Rainis, since poets like Aspazija and Edvarts Virza hatched a historically charged poetry that contributed to the state-building endeavors of Latvia. The two poets' verses focus on cultural advancement and linguistic freedom-two pivotal considerations between a new nation carving out its identity amid Empires. Through the creation of soundscapes-that is, the music-for the words of their poets, the composers reinforce the tools of dissemination, thus strengthening the newly formed visibility of Latvian identity. While that of the composer and the poet is camaraderie within the same story, the partnership of poetry with song was actually developed through a common will: to create an

Alongside assimilating literary symbols, Latvian music also assimilated prevalent visual motifs that were part of production during the time. Visual culture included all the ordinary daily activities (using traditional textiles, wood carvings, painted porcelain, and other handicrafts) that had sacred geometric patterns and representations of flora that had sacred purposes. Composers applied respect to the traditional structures and melodic tropes that they inspired, in their new work. Instrumental pieces were further able to capture movement and moods that were intrinsic to visual touches such as the flow of embroidered patterns or the somberness of the woods.

At the same time, musical environments acted as an inspiration source for visual artists. Painters, illustrators, and sculptors, in particular, found melodic capacities to provide emotional structure in musical works, which allowed them to inject kinetic energy and potential narrative density into their static artistic compositions. The presence of music-branding also took over the amount of representation in the visual landscapes that are representative of national geography and practices. In turn, the physicality of the visual arts helped to build the association strength between compositions as distinctly Latvian, and increase the potential of the audience to connect with both.

As modernism emerged and styles proliferated, the intersection of the visual and musical arenas became especially fecund. Avant-garde/folk artists combined folk traditions with cosmopolitan ways/technology, combining symbolic patterned work with abstract expressionism. Composers were moving in a parallel fashion to marry folk-songs with impressionism and serial/compositional forms. The collaborations among artists and composers put forth new modernist forms in Latvia, developing Latvian national aesthetics amidst a period of burgeoning nationalism, it was also a period of revivalism-like nationalism following independence. Today, much artwork has now turned to references to traditional music or a specific seminal piece in order to reflect and acknowledge the more reciprocal relationship between the visual and musical arts. This is a living tradition, and one that is constantly continuum between both forms of expression- it remains the zenith of Latvian art; a cross-polination of both, the art music domain and folk.

In terms of the artistic communions in Latvian culture, few resonate more solely than music and dances. For thousands of years, there were folk songs that took on rhythmic forms along with seven delicate polka steps for men and women to engage in some courting, or in other words recreational contact, and to acknowledge the feast-day rhythms. Likewise, formal balls would display complex choreography with string or brass ensembles playing war-time dance music. Dance is inherently kinetic, requiring an immutable tempo and a body accustomed to executing repetitive motifs and melodic phrasing, all encoded among people in their bodies through social experience.

Professionally organized groups quickly emerged to provide even more complex productions in combination with Latvian music, with choreography maintaining traditional folk dance elements and movement innovation by borrowing and adapting processes and ideas from dance forms, where elements of indigenous dance and academia became embedded in distinct rhythmic works. Composers, artists alike beginning to expand upon forms, wrote 'suite' like pieces intended to accompany, guide and support choreographed actions. In the 20th century, there was an increase on collaboration between professional dance companies and contemporary composers who recognized a market for substantive multi-dimensional performed experiences. for example, Langsamas brought together modern dance and minimalist sound-based installations to instill current and modern appreciation of Latvian history using hybrid forms.

Today we can see that dance is still strongly shaped by the moods, rhythms and contemporary essence of Latvian music. Dance is also manifested in interpretive companies exploring cultural histories or experimental companies who comment and pay homage to movement forms with hip hop, electronic music and other similar genres to ensure a relationship with culture continues to be relevant for youth. Dance and music have thus maintained a fluid, yet intensely personal, physical and spiritual relationship in the safe space or partnered forum of ongoing discourse about Latvian identity. This entanglement between past and present, mediate and performative forms of cultural codes, speak to the future possibility of sound-space-stories and how culture intersects. Only when key professional intense relationships falter does the essence of cultural codes revert and stratify to drift as an artifact.

The Zemgale region extends westward from the coastline to the hills, and all of it is blessed with grassy plains and gently flowing rivers. Culturally, it descends from the ancient Curonian tribes who exercised its territories. Western Latvian song comes from this agrarian dunescape of lyricism and polyphonic textures; songs built on chromatic solmization that synthesized vocal lines with intricate interlocking patterns.

In terms of lore, the Zemgale folk song was often premised on everyday pastoral life, such as unspoken love and nostalgia for travels, represented lives made by an isolating geography and agrarian rhythm. Pervasively, the lengthly and articulated melodies with gentle ornamentalities shaped a sort of bittersweet pastoral image that became associated with the sad pastoral view of picturesque defect. Alongside these were other unique idiophones like click sticks or Jewish harps and ultimately all could relate in their flexibility or shifting meters and rhythmic spaces and result in a pronounced lilting or fluid quality.

Through the rise and fall of regimes, Zemgale song adapted to the movement of Low and High German settlers but kept its structure. New thematic lyrics also reflected Latvian freedom and state formation in their evolution. Today, through festivals, musicians continue to breathe new life into the living tradition of song and revive oral histories and pre-nationalist styles but often each adds their own beginning to its progress. The bittersweet tone of the region still rings as the gentle soul of Latvia.

Located in the central northwest, Vidzeme boasts ecosystems ranging from coastal areas to thick forest belts, and then to the rising hilly countryside with the characteristics of high/cold mountain pastures farther north. Due to its geographic location at the crossroads of ancient Baltic trade routes, local residents of Vidzeme also experienced the flux of cultural

____

currents that were assimilated into their folk traditions and eventually into their folk song structures.

In famous folk traditions of Vidzeme, a lot of complicated, elaborate instrumental dances became, so to say, the signature style, along with complex interlocking musical parts with shifting rhythmic meters, and strong bouncy sounds from the team of bowed fiddlers. By their very nature, polkas are upbeat, lively, and syncopated, repeating various groups of accelerating rhythms much like the courtship court dances. Most songs featured livelier thematic material that was suggestive of the independent nature of the frontier area—

____

famous feats, games, and adventures.

Not-questionably, Vidzeme melody had influence from the Scandinavian traditions, through Swedish Lutheranizers, but also remnants of Liv traditions, such as boundary-less melodies, parallel chords, and ambiguous harmonic function, who never succumbed to formal melody or rhythm training. In a similar way, polyphony over-all farming and hamlet areas of contrast; but never were more abounding to have this string quartet of music music of four voices (and sometimes five voices). In Vidzeme, sounds take on their own proportional and the audible nature is full of new traditions, yet the distinct sounds lands demonstrate a continually reshape version that will reflect some basic form consistently with the words that followed the landscape of nature in stunning contrast.

Located to the southeast of Latvia, narrow Semigallia boasts warm river valleys and inland plains rich in trees and radiant health, and littered with historical trade routes. Here are myriad cultural intersections that have interlaced slowly over past centuries, like melancholic songs we can hear today. Songs that assimilated the melismas of Orthodox plainsong alongside traditional Baltic elements like the Jew's harp (which has always had a deep history of circulation in this region).

Semigallian folk - and their tradition of folk epics - exhibits an inclination for narrative that required long melodies within a ballad framework of story and legend in song, featuring heroic mysticism. The dances were rhythmically challenging, boasting absorbing asymmetric accents based on the lingering traces of previous centuries Germanic colonists "waltzes." The modes of voice included melodic recitation and euphoric climaxes in chorus, remaining pliable across variable time signatures.

Semigallia is recounted through varied historical vernaculars. In these valleys there are local remnants of dialects to be extracted by social historians. But as well, song sustained an oral history in response to cabin occupants' struggle, unchanged but with three resonant foci; the loves' struggle, or lament, or liberation of rural resistance from transformation both poetic and transcendental filled with emotional, social, and ecological flux—which retains relevance today despite people (including musicians) and markets altering rural life. We hear again only as singers have echoed Semigallian oral epics with contemporary pieces that resurrect melodies from previous generations and cultures paired with modern instruments. The voice of Semigallia continues to break free from the past and celebrate the contemporary heritage, complexities, and traditions of diversity.

Federal research towards sustainably spent fishing in Shore Island, Utah, was conducted in several statewide plans for sustainably managed fishing in Utah, with catch reports showing that half of their stocks met their sustainable limits. Carbon credits and Coastal Restoration credit accounts enabled them to avoid or delay some conservation adoption in the natural resources. But the vast majority of sustainable natural resources in Utah were part of sustainable management because of the activities of local non-profits and individuals. The patterns of the carbon credits systems in Utah are similar in many places: self-provision through other socioeconomic practices and interests. The next step, still unmet or delayed, will be collaboration with Alabama Department of Education to add some transitional strategies to nonsustainable practices using carbon credits to provide additional funding for sustainable development initiatives and transitional strategies.

Folk dances of the region have a heartfelt earnestness and lyricism appropriate to Latgale's agricultural landscape. These polkas have complex asymmetrical rhythms and switches from upbeat, exuberant tempos to slower, contemplative ones. Lyrical ballads overflow with wistful multimorphemic lyrics that relate to religious myths, folk stories and similar themes associated with rural labor.

Latgale somehow maintained its dialect in spite of upheaval and the evolving language of song. Its colloquialisms became saturated in folksong, creating a forum through which historical dialects established in that period survive today, alongside rhythmic instrumental forms of music like the button accordion. Festivals held at sites across Eastern Latvia showcase these particular dialects that together weave a tapestry of musician expression, exhibiting how the oral tradition was a source of regional pride and identity in the face of adversity and despite restrictions and homelessness.

Even centuries of foreign domination coupled with the disapproval of customary behaviours led to indigenous music acting as a hidden mode of maintaining identity and tradition and to encode a complex expression of cultural codes with regard to the oral tradition. Communal singing folk songs provided recent sources of exposure to native dialects and historical perennialism, even in disguised venues. These smaller gatherings also helped forge and strengthen ties of proximity while encouraging an affinity for distinct cultural identification among the efforts of the dominant culture seeking to undermine any semblance of distinctiveness.

Identified within music was a secret, yet powerful, platform to rally static sentiments among movements. Lyrics contained nationalistic and religious subtleties that gave songs subversive degrees of influence to encourage resistance. By creating private places to accumulate and share knowledge through musical traditions, communities strengthened their psychological resilience for committed communal and collective suffering. Though the parasitic nature of persecution reinforced the role music played in attaching identity through the symbolic and spiritual social glue. More than uniting various communities through celebrating covert traditional musical help remind the public of shared injustices and historical hopes for legitimate self-determination, respecting indelible, shared fate. It induced enduring solidarity that allowed people to be useful in the collective development required for that ever cited national resilience.

As dreams of statehood in the late nineteenth-century arose and matured so could music in its unique capacity to advance grass-roots cultural agency and instil national consciousness. Choirs increased as venues for composers to develop musical expressions around new narratives of a connected Latvian identity and nurture artistic acceptance and production. Engagement itself bound or bonded communities together through participation is the act or process of claiming back their cultural self, being proud of who they were as ethnic representatives.

Attending choral events, and song-fests, demonstrated how music could spatially mobilize culture. Mass gatherings on either side of the globe could instigate transnational relationships within communities from the colonies. Musical activities were public symbols to acknowledge ethnic pride for composers, and also demonstrate to a vastly diverse and global audience "This is who we are, come see". Each occurrence of musical activity encouraged collaboration to develop complex arts that represented Latvia, as a new player in contemporary global interactions.

Following independence, music played an important role in civilian state-building processes, as it bound together new social systems from the ground up. Traditional music, and folk music specifically, provided the structures to engage neighbors in collaboration in building national infrastructure and building trust among people. In collaborating to construct a communal barn, workers bonded music structures to physical labor by making labor songs and brought effort and camaraderie together.

The folkdance collectives served the purpose of socializing youth and collectively recounting traditions, ethics and expectations through oral knowledge. Music provided a way for various generations to maintain their relationships in the tumultuous transitions young nations endured to cohere beyond modernization. Folk ensembles provided environments in which diverse peoples participated together to share and celebrate traditions while developing notions of common heritage and community. Along with folk ensembles, song festivals emerged as large demonstrations of community and added as creative expressions uniting people throughout a republic.

Music has been shown to be an essential social adhesive and was ideally surrounded to facilitate social reconstruction to bring peaceful social order. Localized cooperative cultural centered traditions provided mechanisms to begin binding the demobilized young nation from localities experimenting and experiencing a common heritage-based music tradition to act as a national hearth. Musical participation was an agent of interdependence through communal traditions and nurtured communal tradition is evidence of the role music played in supporting social trust. Music helped to promote civic sustainability.

The socially integrative functions of Latvian music remain responsive to today's challenges. Through courses that explore cultural heritage both new and traditional from a creative musical experience, invite individuals to bond and share community cultural codes. Folk ensembles with a global reach enhance a public's shared cultural understanding, and society's development through economic linkages. Festivals of song continue to provide large-scale convergence advertising talent and artistic excellence, importantly reinforce public pride and respect

A new grouping of traditional institutions

supporting modernization and contemporary practices are developing interest within youth demographics. Digital platforms broadening music's social roles when expats participate in virtual choirs globally as well as participating in other discussions. The living repertoire has the agency to mobilize culture, and community roles continues to maintain its prominence through public demands. There is potential for these processes to address broader trends in declining rural populations by becoming a centripetal point in society.

On the whole, the unified roles inherent in Latvian music are as flexible and resilient as the culture it reflects. Demonstrating the ability to foster social cooperation through society's transformations, song-based communities support a nucleus of important substrates, including cultural identity and the development of socially active, culturally connected communities that support flourishing in times of impoverishment and abundance by demonstrating and enhancing social bonds. Drawn from the localized nature of music ability, it brings music in a prime position to assist Latvia with sustaining national advancement.

When understood correctly, Latvian musical traditions are an illustration of the purposes of art that are naturally positive for society.

Through significant periods of challenge indigenous songs untangled the threads of cooperation, shared cultural heritage, and collective resilience against misfortune. It powerfully activated grassroots cultural practices which have been integral to the contemporary national revitalization process. Music is ideally suited as an experiential hearthderived from stabilization through cultivating interdependence and shared heritage and developing the collective capacity to respond to challenges in a unified way.

BEYOND BORDERS

The sounds and tones of Latvian music have reached well beyond the shores of Latvia, penetrating into neighbouring countries and in many cases, the world. The transnational impact of Latvian music proves how timeless and appealing the Latvian musical tradition can be. Musical tradition, by its very nature, speaks to us because of its emotionality and complexity.

The cultural influence of Latvian music is undeniable within the Baltic cultural sphere, especially the neighbouring countries of Estonia and Lithuania. The geographical proximity, historical filters, cultural kinship, and lingering residue of the now-defunct Soviet Union has made for an easy embrace of Latvian styles of music in terms of music composition and music making. The compositions of the Latvian composers resonate deeply within the Baltic notion.

The ease with which Latvian and neighbouring Baltic countries exchange musical styles, has benefitted both the leisure activities of their music making, as well as the cultural mapping of how Baltic cultural entities get intertwined. Thus, the musical creativity in Latvia, Estonia and Lithuania is a painting we all recognize but is always different.

In Estonia, for example, the echo of Latvian music can be experienced from an abundance of cultural festivals and musical partnerships that emphasize the commonality and shared ancestry of the Baltic states. For example, the organization of the Viljandi Folk Music Festival has developed into a mecca for musical ideation, as Latvians frequently play with Estonians on the same stage, creating an inspiring sound and a rythmical telepathy.

Similarly, in Lithuania, the presence of Latvian music has made an impact in the continuous growth of a flourishing folk music scene that is modeled out of the many folk traditions of its northern neighbor. Some of the cultural activities of the Lithuanian National Philharmonic Orchestra have included composers from Latvia in their programming. And with the added emotional model and technical nature of Latvian music, the Lithuanian orchestra has been able to touch their audiences at home and abroad.

While the importance of Latvian music has blossomed in the immediate vicinity of the

Baltic region, the importance of Latvian music has also found itself across the rest of the world. As our societies become increasingly interconnected and different artistic languages can leap over barriers of language, the sound and rhythms of this small nation has simultaneously gained the attention of the world as it continues to find itself on a global stage.

One only needs to look at how internationally renowned are Latvian composers, like Pēteris Vasks and Ēriks Ešenvalds, that have had their music performed by orchestras and ensembles world-wide, to see the successes associated with and provided by the Latvian tradition in various musical forms. Their works are steeped in the ethereal beauty and poetic nature that characterize the Latvian musical tradition, but have also become significant cultural exchanges: their music often becomes collaborative or, at the very least, a cross-cultural exchange.

In addition to their impact in more traditional classical and orchestral contexts, Latvian composers have influenced even more popular forms of culture and popular culture as a whole, and have permeated some popular genres and world music styles. Latvian composers either use or are influenced by the same folk elements and themes, and often include the incorporation of folk melodies and forms giving their works the aura and flavor of world music. In addition, Latvian composers are also present in more innovative and new forms of music through electronic and synthesized works that push the boundaries of sound creation and technology.

In addition to the broader impact of the Latvian tradition, and ultimately the more musical and artistic contexts within neighboring, regional and global geographies, Latvia has also been the site of a unique and interesting series of international or collaborative projects that provide an artistic expression that transcends individual forms and nationalities.

These collaborative projects, which paired Latvian musicians alongside artists of different national and cultural contexts, have led to exciting combinations of musical form and artistic approaches. The creative act of composing what is the storied cultural patterns of Latvia and the musical/performative patterns of other places around the world has given birth to a new and rich artistic vocabulary of the common ground of music. The blending of traditional Latvian folk melodies with the lively rhythms of African percussion-based traditions, or the incorporation of Latvian choral harmonization with the soulful improvisation habits of jazz musicians have undeniably shown that fusion can be a method of creating new art easily.

A strong case of these two modes of collaboration lies in the partnerships of Latvian musicians with collaborators from the Nordic countries, specifically. The related sensibilities and aesthetics have allowed for fertile partnerships because the neighbouring regions represents many of the same cultural and performative activities. There have been concert performances and working together of Latvian composers and performers and their Nordic counterparts.

The outcomes of these partnerships have been truly exhilarating, as the musical milieux of Latvia and Scandinavia have brilliantly combined to create a musical experience that is both comprehensible, and enjoyably exotic. Let me illustrate. The gorgeous bleakness of Latvian folk music has fused beautifully with the nebulous qualities of contemporary Scandinavian music traditions. The result has been musical works that folkloristically reflect on the haggard landscapes that define this elemental place -- the Baltic north.

The mixture of the Scandinavian and Latvian tradition has not only created new, astounding, contemporary art music, but it has also shown itself in contemporary popular music with artists from both traditions developing new, musically hybrid forms that have attracted listeners on a global level. The cultural mix represented by the converging shared practices and resources of Latvians and Scandinavians have enlivened popular improvisatory music, with the rich string-based instrumentation of folk tradition of Latvia meshing rhythmically and digitally with contemporary Scandinavian electronic music. The results have created a sonically hybrid blend that has yet to be categorized into a genre, but, is clearly valued for its celebratory cultural significance in overlapping places!

The collaborative nature of Latvian music, juxtaposed against the creativity of other cultures, is not just limited to the geographic confines of the Baltic and Scandinavian areas, as Latvia and its musicians have strived for possibilities out of the Baltic Sea region, from the very beginning. As a result, the collaborative possibilities are stunning.

An underlined example of such collaborative partnerships can be seen with Latvian composer Pēteris Vasks. Vasks same can be a source for the transportation of ideas across cultures and/or nations through music. His evocative and remarkably emotional pieces created with deep roots in Latvian traditions, are played and admired by ensembles and orchestras around the world. And in many cases, they inspire these relationships to share, collaborate, and continue their conversation through the elements of sound and rhythm.

These international collaborations made a rich spectrum of music possible that is such a specific partnership of unique cultural practices in Latvia, and the universal. The ethereal versatility of Latvian folk music, for example, has resonated across cultures, distinguishable from musical traditions across time and space to greet particular audiences, erasing distance (both cultural, stylistic and place) with this established language of creativity.

Not only has it impacted the sound of collaboration with other nations, and cultures; but visually as well. Global collaboration fuses creative Latvian impulse and functions within multi-disciplinary collaborations, crafting new discourse across visual arts, dance, theater and more. The outcome could become replication unity or creative relations that speak to the creative capacity of the human spirit.

While looking forward and backward into the sphere of Latvian music's influence on creativity in the broader political, social and artistic consciousness of the Baltic (and beyond) will remind you of the power of creativity as a defining, connecting social force in moving across the geographic, temporal and cultural spaces.

The wide-ranging scope of collaborative efforts from other cultures and the sophisticated way that Latvian music has influenced output in neighboring countries and the rest of the world demonstrates clearly that the artistic legacy of a small Baltic country will continue to have its reach across the globe through generations to come.

As the world rapidly shifts towards globalization, with more and more cultural influences moving in and out of everybody's lives, the role and identity of Latvia as a medium for new forms of cultural infusion and artistic representation and expression will only strengthen the role of its creative musical pieces as in-depth reflection of life, art and culture. The exhilaration inherent in the melodies shared across borders and cultures will continue to act as a bridge; increasing collaborations and expression, salt in the curiosity to know everyone's shared experiences of humanity beyond the constraints of language, borders and cultures. Things have shifted to positions we never thought possible before and it's important to embrace the belief that it is possible that it could all happen again.

We cannot overlook the role of Latvia's music culture in a nation's diplomatic efforts as part of the international relations on the global stage. From the first attempts at collaboration on the international stage to the present, Latvia's musical culture has uniquely served as an effective instrument for the building blocks in cultural diplomacy by establishing possibilities through their elements of music (melody and rhythm) between Latvia and the global countries of the continent.

Participate, for example, in the essential mission that Latvian music fulfilled for the country to reclaim their identity and image in a world without the former Soviet Union. Following the end of that relationship, many Latvian musicians and cultural representatives began an important initiative to introduce their programming to the world, using the power of music to create new alliances and reinforce previous relationships.

Latvian music has since had a considerable impact on this campaign, and acts as a cultural vehicle for relationship building and musical exchange, as well as for understanding despite all the physical, linguistic, and ideological distances. Latvian choirs, orchestras, and various performing artists have and continue to perform around the world—from the moment the Soviet Union dissolved to Lionel C. Frenette's global adventure detailed in Tiburtino Moluro's work chapter where they performed with as well as introduced music from both international collaborators and Latvian soloists—through their music, this small Baltic country has made its case for its cultural identity through music, and even nurtured relationships that positively impacted Latvia's diplomatic endeavors.

Latvian music as a part of national state, however, is much more than good opportunity to display artistic talent. There is an evident and symbiotic relationship and interplay of music and cultural diplomacy in Latvia that has produced a rich landscape of cross-fertilization and enhancement where one side nourishes and benefits the other in a constant waltz of political-artistic impulse.

Consider how Latvian music has been utilized as a cultural tool for the advocacy of cultural-political interests abroad. For instance, from purposefully curated programming of Latvian compositions for performance at high-profile international events to the musical ambassadorship of various artists as cultural ambassadors, the music (cultural art) and its unique cultural heritage became an important vehicle for expressing the values, ideas, and identity of the Baltic nation to a diverse global public.

On the other side, the diplomatic considerations that have shaped Latvia's cultural internationalism in turn shaped Latvians music.

The structure of the world elevated the needs of Latvian composers and performers to adjust creatively in real-time in order to connect with numerous international audiences better while generating a deeper understanding of Latvia's cultural identity.

A mutually beneficial relationship between Latvian music and cultural diplomacy has helped establish a nuanced landscape of expression to see through artistic and diplomatic lenses: celebrating the condominal essence and international resonance of music as well as engaging this cultural capital to achieve a strategic national interest through cultural interaction. This reality validates the value of human engagement and authored expressions beyond a conventional diplomacy framework to create interpersonal connections and establish shared meaning and respect for the other, which shifts intellectual comprehension into relational exchange.

Indeed, the sounds and rhythms of Latvia have also become an attraction for minds all over the world, attracting artists, composers, and performers of various cultural backgrounds to participate in an exciting exchange of sound and rhythm. From the incorporation of Latvian folk motifs into the works of internationally recognized artists, to projects that result in radical cross-cultural collaboration, to Latvia's musical traditions have become a source of conjuncture, transcending limits of geography and political ideology.

A particularly striking example of that international collaboration is the work of Latvian composer Pēteris Vasks, whose compositions have become an actual musical exchange between cultures. Vasks' sophisticated and emotional compositions which draw on the traditions of Latvian music, have been taken up by ensembles and orchestras around the world, leading to those international collaborators to enter into an unexpected collaboration of sound and rhythm.

This mutually birthed interaction of internationalities, born through the intermingling of Latvian artistic sensibilities with the energies of other cultures, has also manifested itself in the visual arts, dance, and theater: a beautiful synergy of multidisciplinary expressions that celebrates the very essence of human universality.

With the passage of time, this rich musical tradition of the country seems ever more strongly to have established international bonds, fostered mutual understanding, and developed soft power with reasonable diplomatic outcomes.

Soft power-the notion so famously christened by political scientist Joseph Nye-is when a country creates the ability to shape the preferences of others through the attractiveness of their culture of ideas and values rather than through use of armed threat or economic coercion. Latvia's own musical tradition thus constitutes to put it simply an enormous reservoir of soft power, a cultural resource—the use of which has been strategically directed for enhancing the status of Latvia worldwide and advancing its diplomatic interests.

Consider, for example, the way in which the Latvian repertoire was used as an element in fostering the country's reputation abroad. This way, from a small Baltic country, Latvia evolved into a cultural power whose artistic achievements are respected and admired by the world community. The beautiful performances of Latvian choirs, orchestras, and ensembles on the great world stages offered the country an opportunity to build an international brand outside the limits imposed upon it by its very small territorial and political size, dictating it a cultural leader whose artistic power demands world attention and respect.

And now the political dividends acquired through the soft power of Latvian music go beyond cultural exchange; they also secure political and economic benefits. It is a proven success story of how a nation has used its musical heritage to attract foreign investment, develop tourism, and promote cultural exchanges with some key strategic partners, thus showing the remarkable ability of artistic expression to stimulate broader diplomatic and economic objectives.

Hence, Latvian music's contribution to diplomacy would stand, in any case, as a relish of the everlasting versatility of cultural assets as statecraft instruments. Using the universal nature of musical tradition, Latvia has been able to sculpt a very striking and magical national identity, open to the global sphere, whose powers exerted in the oceans of culture have deviated to an unbalanced irrelevancy in the concrete tangible benefits.

It becomes clear that the position of Latvian music in cultural diplomacy is ready to continue its evolution to further enrich and expand itself, depending upon the shifting environment of the world, and thus placing the nation in the lead of the new paradigm of cultural interchange and mutual understanding.

Indeed, in an age of cultural diplomacy and the recognition of soft power for achieving foreign policy goals, Latvia's musical traditions could serve a larger and more significant role in the country's diplomatic efforts. From how Latvia deploys Latvian artists strategically as cultural agents, to utilizing the same musical tradition processes to build new alliances or deepen the identifiable values of partnership, the songs and sounds of this Baltic state might well become a pillar of its foreign policy.

In addition, changing forms of global connectivity and digital platforms for cultural exchanges, provide new and innovative ways to deploy Latvian music as an element of diplomacy. Such possibilities include reaching global audiences through digital platforms, creating virtual partnerships between musicians in Latvia and abroad, and using social media applications to communicate the nations cultural narrative; all of which could suggest a future where Latvian music holds an even more significant role in Latvia's international relations.

PRESERVING THE LEGACY

The preservation and promotion of Latvian folk music is a noble pursuit that speaks to the very essence of a nation's cultural identity. It is a duty that deserves the very best efforts and attention because with the preservation and promotion of music and culture that has shaped the identity of the people there is a hope for the future that preserves culture and celebrates the spirit endurance of a people.

At the core of the preservation and promotion of Latvian folk music is the Latvian Folklore Archives, a collection of cultural artifacts that represent the origin of the nation's musical identity. It is located in the Latvian Anthropological Open-Air Museum and has a robust collection of field recordings, transcriptions and anthropological work that shows the growth and development of Latvian folk music over time.

The importance and significance of Latvian Folklore Archives can not be overstated - it has been established as a way to preserve and ultimately promote the very essence of a nation's identity, thereby preserving music heritage for the scholarly and musician community, while engaging the public at-large. By cataloguing and ultimately digitising these noted musical resources, the go-between has preserved music and memory to allow its audience to share in the melodies and rhythms heard and sung throughout the Latvian countryside for centuries.

In addition, the Latvian Folklore Archives have changed from simply collection sites of cultural artifacts; they have formed into living archives, and institutions of research and artistic practice, using the extensive repository of folk music of Latvia to engage scholars, musicians, and artists in research and engagement related to the value of using folk music in today's contexts.

With the desire to preserve the musical past of the nation through serious archival projects, Latvia also launched an effort to promote an understanding of folk music and folk traditions, focusing on the need for the young people of the country, who the country's musical future, to appreciate folk music.

Respective music schools and conservatories have led the charge to promote education and engagement with folk music, including the

---

study of folk music in music schools, including by all students the melodies and rhythms of folk music is passed to the next generation of musicians. Through courses, workshops, and by providing learning on access to folk instruments as part of the typical learning repertoire, the music schools and conservatories have developed into strong, visible institutions of Latvian musical tradition and a new generation of practitioners are being engaged in the values of their cultural heritage.

Moreover, Latvian folk music is also being promoted through the wide variety of folk music festivals taking place in Latvia, including the Baltic international folk music festival, which

---

promotes the variety of Baltic musical traditions, the Ligo Summer Solstice Festival, which aligns the musical traits of Latvian folk music with the natural world, and many more festivals around the country. These festivals not only attract audiences from around the country, and further afield, to witness the music, but they also are reinvigorating elements of the past.

The festivals offer live music performance, workshops, and cultural experiences around folk music have played an important role in distributing Latvian folk music and was a way for non-folk enthusiasts to understand and appreciate the music. By allowing people from the community and beyond to engage with the traditions of the past, folk music festivals legitimize, energize, and stimulate present-day Latvian folk music.

The allure of modern music, with its polished production values and immediate accessibility, has created a serious challenge to the viability of Latvian folk traditions. When the surrounding world is made up of modern cultural reference points for young people, those points can overshadow or obscure the cultural touchstones of their forebears that can appear archaic and irrelevant.

Nevertheless, the supporters of Latvian folk music who see its value as a cultural point of reference have not capitulated to modern pressures. Rather, they have pursued a determined course of reinvention and reinvigoration of their tradition, finding new pathways that link their folk tradition with modern voices.

One of the most widely recognized programs has been the Latvian Folk Music Modernization Project a collaboration between traditional musicians and contemporary composers that seeks to explore the dynamic space where the traditional and modern exist. By concurrently creating folk melodies and rhythms, and integrating modern sonic environments that recast the tradition for audiences, these musicians brought new relevance to a distinctively cultural tradition that while recognizing its past, has a present time relevance.

In addition, the resilience of Latvian folk music to modernism is also witnessed in new folk-influenced musical styles, such as exciting combinations of a Lativan folk instrumentation and contemporary electronic music. These styles have had a receptive audience among crossover audiences - especially youth - and illustrate the extant adaptability of Latovanese musical traditions as they shift and develop in relation to and alongside contemporary cultural and artistic expressions.

The success of these efforts can be largely attributed to an intermingled raft of cultural institutions and cultural 'grassroots' organizations working tirelessly to safeguard the country's musical legacy.

At the crest of this commendable venture sit the iconic Latvian National Opera and Ballet, and this national institution's ability to fuse traditional folk music to what otherwise must be, by historical and modern standards, the classical, characteristic of their repertoire is extraordinary. This influential organisation has become synonymous with cultural preservation,while enabling supranational, operatic and balletic productions that have previously unaccompanied the capacity of fusing Latvian folk melodies, rhythms and instrumentation into new creations. It is an admirable that combines tradition and modernism into all-encompassing order - it can and has captivated audiences.

In addition to these prestigious cultural organizations, a dynamic system of community-based organizations has taken root and has become an active player in the cultivation and preservation of Latvian folk music. The Latvian Folklore Society, which has successfully launched a number of documentation and

---

publication efforts to preserve traditional music forms, and the Latvian Folk Music Association, a source for those interested to meet to find ways to foster new creative collaborations and who is also developing future folk music makers/generators, have built a nurturing environment for local folk music, and have contributed to the abundance of both community depth and individual creativity that exists today.

There is a significance that the community-based organizations have beyond preserving Latvian folk music. These organizations act as an important catalysist for the cultivation of fabulous cultural ecosystem, one that respects

---

the relevance of the past while making space for growth in the cross-generational networking of new forms of cultural expression of the 21st century.

Through organizing folk music workshops, hosting community-based festivals, and partnering with educational institutions and cultural centres, these grassroots organizations are teeming grounds for cultural exchange and creative cross-fertilization. It is in such contexts that the songs and rhythms of yesteryear are not only celebrated, but reworked and revitalized with a current hotbed of activity, producing a new wave of Latvian folk music practitioners who are deeply connected to tradition and exuberantly eager for new possibilities.

The music and rhythms that have travelled the Latvian countryside for centuries embody a people's essence, history, joys and sorrows, achievements and challenges, relationship to the land, and breathing rhythms of nature. This cultural expression also transcends time and place to speak to the common human experience in the language of intangible spirit.

People who worked to fulfill this legacy or skill set — the tireless archivists who devoted their careers to documenting and preserving valuable records , the educators who propagated a new generation of practitioners of Latvian folk music, and the tenacious lobbyists who worked within a community to further the idea of cultural preservation — all were working towards the same goals: the satisfaction of watching the tradition of Latvian music and arts endure in the spirit of the music as it was alive from the start; it existed as an important part of the cultural expression of the Latvian people that would be handed down for ages to come.

This legacy, and all it represents, is to be cherished and valued; its place within us is a reminder of an imaginary future world, made narrower through the braided intersections of various human cultures; a world where this country's sounds can send ripples of distance into the minds and hearts of people throughout the globe. These are the legacies we strive to actualize. In doing so we recognize the enduring spirit of a people and the ability of forms of art to transcend time and space.

Latvian musical traditions have been challenged again and again, faced with oppression, wars, and furious waves of modernity. Nevertheless, the persistence of these age-old forms of expression remains, which has preserved cultural continuity and provided national identity and safety for the resilient culture of Latvia.

Think about how Latvian folk music has navigated the whirlpool of adversity in Latvian history. These ancient music traditions have become places of resistance, a site for letting the guard down and safely expressing one's cultural identity against a state that proclaimed the end of national identity throughout the Soviet era when the people of Latvia lived under the constant threat of Russian nationalism and reality.

Confronted with the state's blatant attempts to suppress and destroy their unique musical heritage, the committed stewards of these traditions found unique ways to adjust and to grow. Whether it was the secret creation and distribution of illegal recordings or clandestine folk music events, the Latvian people were committed to preserving the traditional aspects of culture, ensuring the tests of sound and rhythm that kept them alive during years of hardships would live-on through generations.

And following the hard-fought independence movement, as the nation awakened from Soviet rule, the resistance to engage in sameness became even more pronounced. Rather than succumb to the lure of sameness or modernity and abandon the past, the people of Latvia dug deeper into their unyielding musical heritage, recognizing it as an important anchor in reconceptualizing a national identity that had been cruelly sabotaged.

Of course, when they have an enduring capacity to reshape and conceptualize their folk traditions, instead of being defined just by their history, one can understand the lasting power of Latvian music.

In a time where the pressures of globalization have often disrupted cultural identities, Latvian music continues to adapt and be shared, displaying remarkable flexibility and engagement with contemporary cultural phenomena. This repertoire of musical traditions and cultural practices has transcended the routines of everyday practice in a multitude of ways, from folk music being incorporated into the censored work of established pop songwriters to choreographers mixing Latvian rhythm and tunes with the international representations of the music.

One can look to the evocative works of Latvian composers such as Pēteris Vasks whose intensely emotional and relatable compositions have evolved into true vehicles for the exchange of musical ideas from one place to another. Vasks and his peers have been able to simultaneously use what is haunting about folk culture to buoy the technical aspects of new classical compositions often becoming popular in a remarkably unspecific view – a true confluence of national identity, underlying un-revisited history and a musical experience that can be embraced by people, from anywhere and everywhere.

Furthermore, the process of adaptive evolution has also unfolded in the area of digital technology and is illustrated by the way in which the music of Latvia has connected with audiences everywhere. From the ability to distribute recorded performances to facilitating remote collaborations and utilizing social media to showcase its cultural narrative, Latvian musicians have shown awareness of the digital age and how to leverage it so that there would be no loss of relevance or inertia in the ongoing vitality of their music.

As we contemplate the various aspects of adaptability and resilience of Latvian music, we can see that part of the power of these traditions, and why they inevitably continue to captivate audiences in their purity, is not necessarily the history or originality, but the manner in which they will always connect with others across borders.

The unique sound characteristics of Latvian music have emerged as signposts of

---

differentiation during an age when cultural diversity is increasingly eroding. Through both folk song and musicianship, the artistic expressions of this tiny Baltic state have traversed national borders and linguistic borders, that resonated with audiences from various cultures who were drawn in by the musical experience.

Moreover, the international appeal of Latvian music goes beyond the enjoyment of music for music's sake and music for artistic purposes, the long-term effectiveness of these traditions is in their ability to serve as a medium for the human experience and all of its joys and sadness, triumphs and failures, and ties to the land and nature.

It is the incredible ability to emotionally resonate with listeners that solidified the role of Latvian music in the world; to allow listeners with different cultures to connect deeply with music that embodies human yearning in a landscape of distinctly human sounds. In this experience, we get hope for a cultural future without division, where our cultures collide, and artistic expression is a unified tapestry of the human experience.

Latvian music's remarkable survival and adaptability clearly indicate that maintaining and sustaining this cultural capital is important for the country's relevance and viability in the global sphere and it gives them the ability to do this not only as a matter of nostalgia or scholarly interests.

In the melodies and rhythms that have traversed the curls of Latvian countryside for hundreds of years lies the foundation of this nation's identity -- a concentration of its values, the driving connection to its aspirations, and the deep connection to the environment. This is certainly a legacy worth protecting and promoting, not only for the sake of preserving historical practice, but to assure that the special cultural "voice" of Latvia will remain alive within the bodies and minds of generations to come.

To that end, the Latvian people are undertaking a coordinated initiative to protect their musical traditions but are taking up aggressively diverse approaches, initiatives in education, cultural safeguarding and creative innovation.

The music schools and conservatories of the country are at the forefront of this movement, integrating traditional Latvian music study into their degree programs so that the future practitioners have an appreciation of the past and an understanding of how it lives on today. The schools and conservatories have certainly become bastions of Latvian musical tradition producing a new generation of musicians that are committed to carrying on this age-old tradition by offering pertinent coursework, practical workshops, and folk instruments as part of their required repertory.

These educational efforts are also complemented by the creative efforts of the Latvian public to preserve and present their musical legacy through varying archival initiatives and cultural programming. Whether it is the careful transcription and digitization of unique field recordings, or a lively folk music festival taking the public through the nation's unique musical legacies, the display of effort will keep the sound of Latvian history alive today.

Besides, it can be said that the Latvian people have demonstrated great potential to innovate and creatively redesign music traditions by combining the timeless folk legacy of their music with the fresh principles of contemporary music and art, through the creativity of the composers and musicians whose works have successfully married Latvian folk ideas to contemporary popular music, a genre that has caught the imagination and ears of audiences far beyond the everyday sounds of current Latvian artists.

It is this collision of past and present, of tradition and change, that represents the best opportunity, with some likelihood at least, to preserve the legacy of Latvian music. Through the unique and delicate balance that faithful transformation represents, and the slow constant creationist potential of culture, we will help the unique nation of Latvia continue to speak through the music of its past for generations to come.

DISCLAIMER

The publisher and the author are providing this book and its contents on an "as is" basis and make no representations or warranties of any kind concerning this book or its contents. This is a work of nonfiction. No names have been changed, no characters invented, and no events fabricated.

Although the publisher and the author have made every effort to ensure that the information in this book was correct at press time and while this publication is designed to provide accurate information regarding the subject matter covered, the publisher and the author assume no responsibility for mistakes, inaccuracies, omissions, or any other inconsistencies herein and hereby disclaim any liability to any party for any loss, damage, or disruption caused by mistakes or omissions, whether such mistakes or omissions result from negligence, accident, or any other cause.

ABOUT THE AUTHORS

Maher Asaad Baker is a Syrian Musician, Author, and Journalist. He was born in Damascus, Syria in 1977.

Fuad Al-Qrize is a Yemeni Musician, Producer, Author, and Writer, The chief executive officer (CEO) of Al-Qrize Productions.

Copyright © 2024 Maher Asaad Baker

All rights reserved. No part of this document may be reproduced or transmitted in any form or by any means, electronic, mechanical, photocopying, recording, or otherwise, without prior written permission of the publisher.